James Heddon

Success in Bee-Culture

As Practiced and Advised

James Heddon

Success in Bee-Culture
As Practiced and Advised

ISBN/EAN: 9783337144623

Printed in Europe, USA, Canada, Australia, Japan

Cover: Foto ©Andreas Hilbeck / pixelio.de

More available books at **www.hansebooks.com**

SUCCESS

IN

BEE-CULTURE.

AS

PRACTICED AND ADVISED

BY

JAMES HEDDON.

"The earnest desire of succeeding, is almost always a prognostic of success."

INTRODUCTION.

For a number of years past I have been frequently solicited and often urged to write a treatise upon practical bee-culture; but lack of the necessary time for performing such a task, has hitherto prevented. I had hoped, however, that an opportune time would come, when, free from business cares, I might comply with this oft-repeated request. In the steady, changeless lapse of time, the years have come and gone, and this dream has not materialized, with no prospect of a suitable opportunity for such a consumation; and so at intervals, amid the pressing cares of business I have here and there, jotted down some facts and thoughts pertaining to our pursuit, which, I trust, may not be without value to those for whom they have been written. In the delineation of methods of management, and of implements and devices, appertaining thereto, it has been my constant aim to present such only as will approximate uniform and unvarying success, as nearly as possible, when the requisite conditions have been complied with, and thereby obviate the disappointments and vexatious losses, resulting from the complicated and impracticable in both management and utensils. In short, the instruction herein given, is from the dollar and cent basis—the financial results to accrue therefrom, and not from the vagaries and inconsistencies of empiricisms, aiming to present the new and useful rather than mere repetition of the old. I have not aimed in these pages, to treat of all the minor points pertaining to our pursuit, but have endeavored to elucidate those that are vital to our success, many of which I believe have not hitherto received their due share of attention; hence it is not claimed to be a work especially adapted to the beginner in apiculture. Firmly believing that our ranks are already sufficiently full, for the welfare of the fraternity, I have written more especially to promote the success of those already possessing some knowledge of bee management, than to persuade the addition of recruits; and, to the attainment of this end, have traversed some hitherto neglected fields, in the interest of the specialist. I have earnestly sought to be of some service to this class, in a way I think neglected by my predecessors in apistical literature.

This little book is not designed to take the place of any of the excelcent works upon apiculture that we already possess, but rather to supplement them in such themes as seem to have been inadequately treated, from the standpoint of my own experience. It has been well said that "a house that contains a library has a soul." Our pursuit borders upon the professional, more so, perhaps, than most of the business avocations, and yet all the books devoted to bee-culture, combined, do not make a tithe of the professional library. We need them all to direct us in the pathway that leads to success. I have aimed to make this pathway less obscure, by specialty in treatment of such themes as my own experience has demonstrated to be vital to success in honey production—the ultimate end of bee-culture. I have only briefly touched natural history, etomology, botany and kindred topics which are so ably and fully elucidated by Professor A. J. Cook, in his "BEE-KEEPERS' GUIDE" and in Mr. Thomas G. Newman's "BEES AND HONEY." I know of no work upon bee-culture, however unpretentious, but that is worth many times its cost to the owner of an apiary, be its number of colonies ever so small.

In this attempt at embodying some of my ideas and conclusions in book form, forced upon me by a somewhat varied and extended experience, I cannot hope nor expect to escape criticism: I do not desire it. I court the fullest investigation and all honest criticism from any and every source. But, before condemning its recommendations I would most respectfully suggest a thorough and impartial trial of the same. Remember that everything herein given based upon my experience, whether of method or device, has been a success with me, and will succeed equally well in the hands of all, if directed by even a moderate degree of tact and skill. While excluding all advertisements from the covers of this book, I have freely recommended such goods, belonging to others, as have proven of value, in my own apiaries, having given in every instance manufacturer's address; and have thus endeavored to keep the interest of the apiarist paramount, regardless of other considerations. In this connection I wish to acknowledge my indebtedness to a member of the bee-keeping fraternity, who has rendered valuable assistance in the preparation of this volume. Being conversant with each other's operations, and having conducted much the same line of experiments through a series of years, accounts in a great measure, for the similarity of our conclusions respecting the essential problems with which we have had to deal. As he is somewhat averse to publicity, I shall speak of him in the following pages as "My Friend." His lucid style, careful observation and thorough knowledge of the business, will, I feel sure, be at once conceded by the reader. In addition to those specially mentioned throughout these pages to whom I feel indebted for valuable ideas and devices, and outside of my own experience of seventeen years of practical life in the apiary, I wish to express my deep sense of gratitude for ideas and suggestions received from any and every source, whether from members of the fraternity in social converse or at bee-conventions or from books or periodicals devoted to practical bee-culture. I wish to give full credit here in order to save both repetition and space in the body of the work itself.

In writing a practical work for the guidance of my brother bee-keepers, I refer with pardonable pride to the fact that my financial success has been attained entirely within the domain of bee-culture; that in this little book I have laid down a definite, tangible system of management perfectly adapted to either the perfected movable frame, or those now in general use. In doing this I have not aimed at immediate popularity, but rather for the welfare of those who need assistance and for whom I have struggled for the past ten years, confident that the future will fully verify my position.

Hastily and imperfectly written, with no attempt at elegance of diction, flowery sentences or rounded periods, but simply to direct those who are striving to earn an honest livelihood with bees, to better results, this little unpretentious work is submitted by the author.

JAMES HEDDON,
Dowagiac, Mich.

PREFACE.

There seems to be a growing tendency of late years, for authors of books upon practical subjects to begin by apologizing for the performance of such a work. In this respect I must differ, inasmuch as I have no apologies to offer. None are needed. No man who has a truth to tell, that needs to be told, should apologize for its utterance. This "apology business," as I view it, implies also, a supposed excellent performance by the author—a position having conceit for its basis and superstructure. It does not suit me, and if expected by the public, I beg to be excused.

There are three motives that are claimed to actuate the author in the production of a book, pertaining to the affairs of life:

1. The philanthropic, which excludes self, and simply seeks to benefit others.

2. The purely selfish, which does not consider the welfare of the reader, but only desires self-aggrandizement.

3. The belief that there may be an open field for mutual benefit—a pecuniary advantage to both author and reader. To this latter class I belong. I do not, for one moment, wish it to be understood, that self-interest has been entirely laid aside; but while my own interests are advanced, I hope to enhance the reader's, also. In the very nature of things, a book of practical value must be mutually advantageous. This is my hope and desire—the future will determine its fruition.

I trust I may say without egotism, that my efforts in the past to make honey production as a specialty reasonably remunerative, have been fairly successful. The eager questioning that has resulted from this, respecting both method and device to secure favorable financial results, has convinced me that success, or the lack of it, in honey production, vitally affects the "bread and butter" question, with many others as well as myself. To this class I have addressed myself, with whatever degree of ability I may possess, earnestly hoping to be of some service in lightening their anxieties and burdens in the journey of life.

To oft-repeated inquiries I have replied—"I will write a book upon bee-culture, when the wintering problem has been solved." The disastrous losses in wintering have, hitherto, rendered our pursuit an extra hazardous one; but a perusal of the chapter on "Wintering" will show the reader, that at last, I feel confident that we stand upon solid ground.

If there be any one branch of apiculture in which I feel proficient, it is the mechanical. To this subject in general, and hives in particular, I have devoted almost unremitting thought and constant experiment. My zeal to secure a hive that would be as nearly automatic as possible, requiring the least possible amount of manipulation, simplifying and systematizing the labors of the apiarist and enable him to attain the best aggregate results in honey production, is fully attested by almost numberless castaways in my museum of condemned hives. But I am happy to add, that the dreams and hopes of over eighteen years, seem now to be realized. See chapter on hives.

"He who steals bread may have an excuse, but he who purloins the ideas and inventions of another, is a thief by nature." In this sentiment I fully concur, and I have endeavored to give due credit to any and every source from which I have drawn. If there are any exceptions to this, it is simply an oversight, for which I will be thankful for correction.

In the performance of this not altogether self-imposed task, I have endeavored to faithfully and impartially maintain what I conceive to be the right, regardless of individual interests. Whenever the interest of the individual has clearly seemed to me to run counter to that of the fraternity, I have not hesitated to criticise, fairly and judicially, I trust; where the interest of the individual promotes that of the public, I have tried to freely accord merited praise.

CHAPTER I.

Bee-Keeping as a Business.

Perhaps there is no branch of agriculture about which there has been entertained so much superstition, as concerning apiculture.

The days of ignorance and false notions concerning bee-keeping, more especially its results, are by no means past. When I began the business as a specialist, fifteen years ago, I was told by many friends and neighbors that I certainly could not succeed in making a living from the results of "bees." "The bee business!" "The bug business!" Numerous were the instances of failure of "my father, down in Ohio;" "Uncle Levi, in New-York state;" "A cousin of mine back in Pennsylvania," etc., etc., offered to encourage me on my lonely way, for at that time I was, I think, the only specialist in Michigan, and there was hardly enough of us in the United States to make a quorum. Since that time many have demonstrated that with natural tact, and a knowledge of the theory and practice of the pursuit, honey producing can be made a business, capable of supporting him who embarks in it.

Some of our brotherhood who had much more imagination and enthusiasm, than practical knowledge of the business, used to tell us that "bees work for nothing and board themselves." We have also heard that "farming is the best of all avocations." "Crops grow nights and Sundays, when the farmer is asleep." That "all one needs to do, is to get some ground, just run a plow through it, drop in the kernels of corn; when they sprout, tickle said sprouts a little with a hoe, and go out in autumn when the glorious sun is shining and gather in the golden ears." Both stories have some truth in them, and I leave you to guess, how much. In all lines of production, conditions seem to have been so fixed that the producer must earn all he gets. That nearly every new invention, by means of which pain and cost of production are lessened, redounds in most part, to the interest of the consumer, by lessening the price of the article produced. I will call your attention to one such instance in our own business. Take the honey extractor, for instance. The product when properly handled, was found to be excellent, and for one or two years brought in market, nearly, or quite as much as honey in the comb. This condition of affairs soon ended, the price in latter years being steady at just one-half of that of comb honey in the general markets.

Allow me to go back long enough to tell you that those friends who advised me to keep out of the "bug business," saying that it could not be made a business, made one other equally sad mistake at the same time. They said: "O! You can keep a few colonies in your yard for your own use, with pleasure and profit." Now, do you not know from the experience of the past, that less pleasure and profit has been derived from the " few colonies of bees " kept on the farm, than from anyother branch of mixed husbandry, when taken all in all, one year with another ? I think I know that this is a fact, as a rule. Before the advent of modern improvements, there was more reason for the " few colonies for our own use " than at present, because honey producing as a successful specialty, was well nigh impossible, while under the present regime—scarcely any business under the sun is better adapted to, or more necessarily confined to specialty, when looked at in a dollar and cent point of view. A large part of the necessary capital and labor must be of; and devoted to, mechanics, and in all this line has specialty done so much for us, that we are tempted to ask the counter-storekeeper, where he stole those articles on the five, ten and twenty-five cent counters.

Let us pause to consider the great advantages of specializing, not only in apiculture, but any line of business. Let me quote from Mr. T. B. Terry, of Hudson, Ohio ; a clear thinker and forcible writer, and one who has gained a world-wide reputation, as well as a competency, as a specialist in potato culture :

" The day has passed when there is any necessity for such a diversity of crops—when it is necessary for a man to raise almost everything he wants, on his own farm. It was necessary once, when the country was new, and there were no railroads markets, and not much money; but now let it go, to a certain extent, along with the stage-coach and scythe, and let us improve in this respect as much as we have in our means of communication and in our agricultural implements. And we are improving. For example, look at the cattle-raisers on the great plains, the wheat-growers of the Northwest, and the corn-farmers of the West. These men are specialists, and they are sadly crowding the old mixed farming of Ohio and the East. And it is being gradually crowded at home by enterprising specialists, such as the fruit-grower, the dairyman, and the market farmer.

When I speak of the potato-grower as a specialist I do not mean that he should grow just potatoes and nothing else, but, rather, that he should make that his leading crop—his main source of income. Other crops must be grown with them, of course, to make up a rotation and to keep the land up by having something to feed out to stock.

That pithy little paper, OUR COUNTRY HOME, expresses just my views on the subject of specialties. Let me quote a few lines :

' Division of labor is one of the grandest ideas of this grand nineteenth century, and it is just as grand on the farm as it is in the factory or workshop, in business, art, or scholarship. This world is too big for one man to do all that there is to be done in it, or to compass its entire store of knowledge. " That it is better to do one thing at a time, and do it well," is truer to-day than ever before, and as true on the farm as off from it. Find out what you and your farm can do best, and then do it, but don't try to do everything. You can't be a market-gardener and a mule-raiser at the same time, and expect to achieve eminence in either direction. You need not expect to grow potatoes as does Terry, and steers as does Gillette, on the same land, and arrive at the distinction from which they now complacently look down on common mortals. Vick would never have been Vick, had he undertaken to grow pork and flower-seed together. Take your text, and stick to it. Choose your branch of farming, and follow it up ; so shall you prosper.'

Now for some reasons why the large grower of potatoes, who makes this his chief business, can make more money. First, he can afford to have all the tools that are made for saving labor, and taking the best of care of the crop, and marketing it in nice shape, such as a planter, smoothing harrow. special cultivators and horse-hoes, bushel boxes, spring-wagons, etc. The man who raises only two or three acres cannot afford all these expensive labor-saving tools, and therefore cannot make as much money for he cannot put in or care for his crop as cheaply, nor can he market it in as nice shape. Again, the specialist can not only have the advantage of all the best tools, but, what is still more important, he can use them just when they ought to be used, as that is his business, and there is nothing else to interfere. With a great variety of crops to care for, and perhaps a dairy besides, this is often quite impossible. There are times, in this locality, when a single day's work with the whole farm force, each man with a cultivator and horse, just exactly at the right time, would be of very great advantage to the crop—possibly almost the making of it. The specialist can put in that day's work. Also the large grower has a chance to concentrate most of his energies and study in one direction, rather than scatter them thinly in many directions. Instead of being a Jack at all trades, and particularly good at none, he can have a chance to excel in one direction. If he will improve that chance, and push his specialty to the utmost, he will find that it not only pays in dollars and cents, and develops his thinking faculties, and makes more of a man of him, but he will get rid of a great deal of the worry, as well as loss, of having too many irons in the fire. * * * * *

We buy everything we want, except potatoes, milk, and a little garden stuff. We do not fuss to make our butter, even, but rather eat the cream on berries which some specialist has raised (of course, we raise our own hay for the horses and cows). There isn't a pig nor a chicken, a calf nor a colt, a bee-hive, a sheep, nor even a dog on my place; so you see I practice what I preach—or, rather, I am preaching what I have practiced for years, and found to be the easiest way for me to make a good living with the least worry, from my farm, and I find it the pleasantest way too. There is a pleasure about doing one's level best, as the specialist has a chance to do, and then the profits are great. Could any man living support a medium-sized family, and live comfortably, pay his hired help liberally, and all other running expenses, and get ahead over a thousand dollars a year, actual cash saved, from thirty-six acres of plow land and nineteen acres of poor pasture, by following ordinary mixed farming? I couldn't. I could hardly live, let alone getting ahead any. * *. *,

'You mustn't have your eggs all in one basket.' But those words do not scare me at all. That saying belongs to the days when Ohio was the 'Far West,' and it took almost all summer to go out there and back. If a man raised too much of one thing, then he was in a bad fix on account of the poor facilities for exchanging, and the lack of markets and the scarcity of money. But, how different it is now! The whole world is one market to-day. We can sell almost any thing for cash, and with the cash we can buy almost any thing we want, right at our doors.

Of course, we specialists must expect reverses—all kinds of business are subject to them; but my experience has been, thus far, that the reverse years, or years when the crop was almost a failure, were the years when I made the most money. Why? Simply because I had just that one thing to do, and I did it. I looked out for the eggs that were all in one basket. The men with eggs in many baskets said, 'Never mind if we do drop one or two; we will get through with some of them.' I walked carefully and got through with all of them, and got a big price because the other fellows broke so many."

The nature of apiculture is such, that it is eminently adapted to specialty. It has little connection with farming. While it would be unwise for him to do so, the blacksmith could more profitably add a small apiary to his business, as he could, during the dullest season for smithing, handle his bees when they most need it; and watch for the issuing of swarms, from his shop window.

Regarding apiculture as a specialty, what are the prospects for him who would embark? I do not see how they can be bad. Let us take a look at the two influencing factors outside of the ability of the operator, namely : supply and demand. The price of all produce fluctuates or ebbs and flows, like the tide of the ocean, sometimes above and sometimes below cost of production.

The product, honey, cannot escape this law. My own opinion is that just in the near future we may experience a reaction, from a few years' excellent prices, recently passed through, but the immutable law of action and reaction so well known to you all, will keep it hovering about the cost-of-production point, the same as does all other products.

Now, regarding supply, I doubt if one-twentieth part (possibly it would be correct to say one-hundredth part) of the honey annually secreted by the flora of the United States, is ever gathered by bees. I feel very confident that the time is far distant, if ever to come, when it can all be gathered at a profit. There are at present many unoccupied areas waiting for the future apiarist. Whether he can work any of them at a living profit or not, depends mainly upon his personal ability.

To all those now in the business, or thinking of engaging in it, I wish to impress upon your minds the immense importance of occupying a field or area, entirely clear of all other bees; many of the reasons for which, will be given under the head of "Over-stocking." It is my opinion that the supply of honey, now produced in the world, is fully equal to the demand, and I can find no reason for inducing those occupied in other pur-. suits, to embark in its production, much less to dabble with a few colonies. It would be criminal for me to hold out fictitious inducements for those who are failing in other lines of business, to try ours. To succeed as a honey producer, requires that amount of tact and industry, that will succeed at almost any other calling.

Knowing that I shall incur the opposition of a few other writers, and perhaps have little aid from anyone except "Father Time," I am forced to say that I do not consider bee-keeping adapted to the gentler sex. I do not dispute the fact, that there are some women that can succeed as honey producers, the same as some succeed as pedestrians, hostlers, farmers, stock-raisers, etc., etc., but that the nature of the work as carried on in an apiary where honey is produced at minimum cost, is adapted to women, I cannot believe. I certainly do not want my daughter to try to compete with men, in this labor. Let us remember that the same inexorable law prevades all classes of production, viz.: He who produces at maximum cost, will fail. He who produces at minimum cost, will succeed.

CHAPTER II.

Natural History.

We are told, the honey-bee is an Articulate (composed of joints), of the class Insecta, sub-class Hexapoda, the order Hymenoptera, family Apidæ, the genus Apis, and the species Apis Mellifica. Of the several varieties, we have to deal with only two—the German, or black bee and the Italian, or, as sometimes called by its European name—Ligurian.

PHYSIOLOGY.

A normal colony of bees consists of a single queen, or mother bee, many thousand workers (neuter bees) and at certain seasons, drones (or male bees).

The queen (readily distinguished by her peculiar, elongated appearance) when fertile, lays the eggs from which all the bees of the hive are produced. Her capacity when properly developed, with favorable conditions, is from two to four thousand eggs per day. The eggs laid in worker cells, hatch into larvæ in three days, are fed and sealed over in five days more, and hatch in about thirteen days thereafter, or twenty-one days from the laying of the egg by the queen. These same eggs, differently treated, will produce queens, being, like the workers, capped over five days from hatching into larvæ—or eight days from the time the eggs are laid—but come forth from the cell in eight days more, or sixteen days from the egg. While this is the rule, the exceptions are numerous. I have repeatedly known from eighteen to twenty-two days to elapse between the laying of the egg and the hatching of the queen, and in one instance, the time was extended to a full twenty-five days. The bees seem to possess the power to retard the development of both eggs and larvæ, as also to hasten this process, by shortening the time nearly one day. The cells in which workers are reared, measure about five to the inch; the drone cells are larger, measuring four to the inch, and nearly horizontal, and are hexagonal, or six sided. Queen cells usually approach the perpendicular, in position, (but may be horizontal or any angle between it and the vertical) are larger and longer than drone cells, nearly round in form, and taper toward the lower or outer end. The drones are slowest in devel-opement, maturing in about twenty-four days. The office of the queen is egg-laying, only; the worker bees nurse and cap the brood, build comb, gather honey and pollen, store the same in the combs, and seal it over, and ventilate, and defend their hives against enemies. In addition to performing the office of the male, the drone augments the heat of the hive required for breeding, and I fully believe, in some way, assists in the evaporation or "ripening" of freshly stored nectar. The queen becomes fertilized in the open air, when from five to ten days old, (although this may be retarded by bad weather or other unfavorable circumstances) and commences her duties of laying, in about two days thereafter. She lives to be from one to four years of age (and in isolated cases, still longer) but the period of her greatest usefulness is often compassed within two years.

The age of the worker-bees, varies greatly with the season of the year; from one to eight months. I believe however, from years of careful observation in the apiary, that their average duration of life in the honey season, does not exceed forty-five days. Such at least, holds true of my own locality. They begin active operations in honey gathering when from four to eight days of age, and continue until their almost ceaseless industry has brought on the period of decrepitude and decay.

Owing to the casualties by which they are surrounded, the age of the drone is an uncertain quantity. Even though they were not liable to be slaughtered by the workers at almost any moment, (in colonies normally conditioned) I believe them to be short lived. Although performing no laborious work, and requiring a longer period for their developement than either queens or workers, circumstances point unmistakably to an evanescent life. In my own location, where we often have a late honey-flow, I have repeatedly known them to go into winter quarters with the bees, and yet I have never, in even a single instance, been able to discover a live drone, the following spring, or even during any warm time that allowed the bees a mid-winter flight.

The above. I believe, embodies the essential features of this theme, as applicable to practical bee-culture. We are often reminded of the wondrous processes of nature, to secure unvarying results, and of the wise and beneficient adaptation of means to conserve desired ends. While it is true that we may not violate nature's laws with impunity, it is equally true that she is simply a blind force, caring naught for our wishes and desires. Experience has clearly shown many of her processes to be faulty, and, undirected by man, often defeats the cherished results he is striving to gain. It is becoming more and more evident, with the lapse of years, that the mental horizon of man should be freed from the misty fogs of superstition, if he would behold in all their force and beauty, the shining stars of truth in the realms of the useful and practical.

CHAPTER III.

Varieties of Bees.

For the class I am writing, I need say nothing of the genders of our common honey bees. I wish to deal with the different races and strains of bees, that most honey producers are now using. I have never tested the merits of Cyprian, Syrian or Carniolan bees, as the reports from those who have been experimenting with them, have cautioned me against bringing any of that blood into my locality, well knowing how much easier it is to introduce, than to entirely eliminate foreign blood.

In giving you my conclusions, upon the above subject, conclusions formed from continued careful experiment with German and Italian bees, of the various strains, and observation and conversation with friends who have experimented with Cyprians, Syrians and Carniolans, I will say that I believe that all these so-called races should properly be divided into two —the brown and yellow bees; of which I believe the Italian and German represent the best of the two classes. Now, if one race possessed all points of superiority, and the other none of them, any discussion regarding "best bees," would be a thing of the past; but as it is a fact that points of superiority and inferiority, are about balanced between the races, it leaves a wide field in which the apiarist may well use his judgment and tact.

I think all practical honey-producers will admit that the following points of differentiation between the two races, not only illustrate more radical differences, but points of more importance.

Let us mention of the yellow bees, the following valuable points of superiority:

1. Protection of their home against enemies. This characteristic is of greater value to the novice than the specialist; or, to those living in the South, gaining no assistance from severe winters.

2. As a rule, they have a longer proboscis. This point is of advantage in such locations as, at certain times of the year, abound with flowers which have many nectaries pretty deep for honey-bees.

While it is more or less correct to say that the Italians stick better to their combs, are more courageous, will remain in any new location better, are less liable to quarrel when different colonies are united, though fiercer in disposition, are less liable to sting, because they are less liable to take wing, that the queen is more readily found, etc.—all these are minor points, and even the second, can hardly be called a major point.

In 1883, Mr. A. W. Osborn (now a large honey-producer of Cuba) penned the following, for the AMERICAN BEE-JOURNAL;

"While the praise of the different races of bees—the Italians, the Holy Lands, Cyprians and others is being sounded far and wide; and while the best talent of our country is being engaged to bring more prominently before the public the superior qualities of the above named races, there are but few that have the boldness to come forward and advocate the good traits of character of the German bee (not the black). I know that one who has the independence to advocate the good qualtiies of the German race of bees, must expect to call down upon his head the scorn, disapprobation and disgust of the great mass of bee-keepers of to-day.

Let us go carefully over the ground and see if the German bees have not some traits, that the honorable bee-keeper is bound to respect. In the first place they excel as comb builders; they excel as rapid workers to draw out foundation; they excel as pioneers to strike out from the brood-chamber (and out of the queen's way) to store their honey; the queens thus having no honey to bother them, can fill the combs from top to bottom, and from end to end; they excel in keeping their hives full of workers to gather the crop; all other conditions being favorable, they excel as non-swarmers, when you give them plenty of room..

While I would not wish to be understood that I think the German bee possesses all the good traits to be desired in the "coming bee," yet I would wish them to have credit for what good there is in them; and that their good qualities shall not be ignored when looking around for material to make up that long-looked-for APIS-AMERICANA. I am satisfied, from my own experience, that the crossing of the different races makes better business-bees than either, bred pure."

Mr. George Maloney, a very intelligent man, well versed in history and general science, as well as apiculture, on page 118, of the BEE-JOUR-NAL, for 1885, makes an unanswerable argument favoring the crossing of our different races and strains of bees.

Is it not true of the brown German bees:

1. That they are superior comb-builders, making wax more readily, of better color, capping over their combs quicker and whiter, leaving a space between the honey surface and cap which not only much improves the appearance, but enhances the price two or three cents per pound, securing a more ready sale with that advance, and enables the honey to bear a humid atmosphere for a considerable time, without any material deterioration.

(The foregoing was of not so much importance twelve and fifteen years ago, when the honey supply was unequal to the demand and buyers came hundreds of miles to secure our crop—let it look as it might, if it was only "honey;" but, in these days, it is to me the most important point of superiority to be found with any race of bees.)

2. They are much less inclined to swarm. This is an important trait, especially to the larger special producer; also to any who cannot give their apiaries close attention; either because they have too many apiaries for the help employed, or too few colonies in one apiary to afford them continual attention.

Minor points of superiority are, that they build the most worker comb and straighter (some may wonder why I call straight worker comb-building a minor point. Because of the otherwise, wise and general use of full sheets of comb foundation; but in cases where such are not used, this trait of the brown German bee is a major point, greatly in their favor), enter surplus receptacles more readily, in cases where the apiarist has bad communications thereto, are more easily shaken from the combs (sometimes an advantage and other times not), and are more sensibly affected by loss of queen. (This aids us in many manipulations.)

When swarming, these bees alight sooner and with more certainty, than Italians; a swarm hives more readily, they can be driven more easily, heeding the admonitions of the smoker more promptly, etc.

I do not doubt the wisdom of choosing the pure Italian bees, by those who live in the South, and make extracted honey a specialty; but for those who live in the North, and produce comb honey (which I think more profitable wherever the bulk of the crop is light colored), my experience forces me to recommend the brown German bees, or crosses between them, and the leather-colored Italians. (The small, black variety of Germans, should be avoided, because of their nervous, irritable nature).

About eight years ago I conceived the idea that I could, by controlled crossings, produce a strain (not race) of bees (using these two races for material to work with) that would possess more of valuable characteristics than either race in its purity.

I began by rearing queens from pure Italian mothers, of the longer and larger leather-colored variety. These queens were mated with drones of the larger brown variety of German bees and by continued selections from these crosses, I have succeeded in establishing a strain, that very many of our practical honey producers, as well as myself, consider greatly superior to pure Italians, for the production of comb honey. I believe that all my students who have handled these bees, concur in the above sentiment. While I have kept all the valuable traits of the Italians, I have not succeeded in retaining all those of the German bees, in the highest degree, but as a general-purpose bee, I, this day, much prefer them to any other race or strain of bees, with which I am acquainted.

While I am willing to pit colony for colony of this strain, against an equal number of Italians, for steadfastness to the combs and consequent good behavior; longer tongue, and consequent honey-gathering qualities, and faithful protection of their home against all enemies, I cannot truthfully say that they will compare favorably with some colonies of the best strains of pure German bees, in the one point of snow-white capping of their surplus honey.

Because accidental Hybrid bees, have borne a reputation for stinging, I am often asked if my new strain of crosses are well-behaved. I answer yes, and the reason is because I have carefully preserved that steadfast clinging to the comb, so characteristic of the pure Italians. The yellow races of bees are more courageous and belligerent than the dark bees, but as bees sting after taking wing, and as ten times more brown bees than yellow ones take wing when opening hives, etc., we get the most stings from crosses which inherit the temper and courage of Italians and loose-footedness of brown or black bees. See that these crosses inherit the tendency to remain steadfast upon the comb, and you have the best dispositioned bees in the world. This is not only clearly logical, but is practically proven by the actions of one of the yellow varieties, that readily leave their combs like dark bees, and have the true yellow disposition; viz.: The Cyprians, which are admitted to be one of the most belligerent races of bees, known. It is also demonstrated in my own apiary.

New conditions and demands, force us to different fixtures. In many things, I find that what was best fifteen years ago, (and would be to-day, were conditions the same) are not best for the present. I am convinced that there is going to be a turning backward from the yellow to the brown bee. We are as yet little acquainted with the Carniolans; should it prove that this strain is equal to the Germans (if nothing more), the change would likely be done by introducing them.

Purchasers of queens prefer something new; vendors prefer the new prices. This branch of the darker race is already being praised (above the Italians) for the same qualifications possessed by the brown Germans. It is however, further declared, that they excel all in good nature; but what, to me, more than off-sets that, is an accompanying admission that they are as bad or worse than the Italians about swarming.

To close, I will say that if you are producing comb honey exclusively, or nearly so, and have a good strain of brown bees, do not be in haste to change them. If you live in the South, and raise extracted honey mainly, pure leather-colored Italians are perhaps the best bee that you can get. On the other hand, if you have any reason to introduce new blood into your apiary, and wish a comb honey, or general-purpose bee, you will find judiciously bred crosses between brown German, and leather-colored Italian bees, most excellent workers, comb-builders and well-behaved.

CHAPTER IV.

Value of Bees.

A standard of value of bees, that would remain a standard or fixed price, cannot be given. Much depends upon the necessities of the owner and purchaser, as well as upon the price of their products. Again, the difference between spring and fall value depends upon our ability to carry our bees safely through the winter. Much also depends upon the kind of bees and hives, the condition of the combs, etc. I consider a well-bred, normal colony, in a preferred modern hive, with straight combs, at present, worth in the spring, eight dollars. I think them better worth that amount, than common bees in box, or objectionable frame hives are worth three dollars. Bees are sold in bulk, at from one dollar to two dollars per pound, according to the time of year, kind of bees and supply and demand.

QUEENS

that are one or two years old and tested for valuable qualities are usually sold at two to three dollars each, according to the time of year; those sold earlier in the season bringing the higher price. Queens reared and sold as soon as they are fertile and have begun to lay, without much knowledge of their characteristics, bring one dollar each and are called "dollar queens;" though they are often sold early at one dollar and twenty-five cents each, and later, in quantity at ten dollars per dozen.

For those who do not wish to rear queens at all, but desire some fertilized ones to use, I recommend the dollar queen, if properly reared; for all those who rear their own queens, I cannot be too persuasive in advising them to purchase only selected, tested queens to breed from.

CHAPTER V.

Bees on Shares.

" What are just terms for taking bees on shares—just to the owner and operator?" is a question that has many times been asked me, both privately and publicly. At this time I do not know of any better answer than the one I gave Mr. Thomas, of Ohio, when answering the questions sent to the question department of the AMERICAN BEE-JOURNAL, for 1883, and I will quote it in its entirety from page 289:

"The " Bees on Shares " question, is one that I have studied considerably. In answering the above, I do so with a prejudice in favor of the laborer versus the capitalist, a principle herein involved, though on ever so small a scale. Here are two facts:

. 1. Bees are to some considerable extent a risky property; their life and the amount of their stores being an unknown quantity. One should have a larger per cent. of income from such property, by three or four fold, than from a good, safe real estate mortgage.

2. On the other hand, the laborer should have an average income in advance of the ' going wages.' All this can be realized from the manipulation of bees, provided the bees are in proper hives, in a good location, and the work done by a faithful and learned man, and directed by experience and tact.

I will lay down the following terms as those which seem to me the nearest to being just and the best adapted to both parties.

The one owning the bees shall furnish the place to establish the apiary. He shall furnish all the fixtures in every respect. The laborer shall furnish himself ; nothing more.

> The laziest tramp can turn and mend,
> And be a man " for a' that."

The capitalist furnishes bees, apiary, tools, new hives for increase, comb foundation for surplus and brood departments, sections, shipping crates, and everything including advice suggested by his riper experience (which, it is supposable he possesses). He shall have the diction of the general plan of management, while the rentor does all the work and is dictator of the detail manipulation. The division shall be as follows :

Each party shall have one-half of the surplus honey, and when it is sold, each one shall pay one-half cost of sections, shipping crates and surplus comb foundation that is sold with the season's crop. The capitalist shall have diction over the whole crop, merely dividing the money for the same unless the laborer gives security for the payment of his half of the sections, foundation and crates, when the honey may be divided, and each sell his own as he chooses. The bees should be managed for securing the greatest amount of surplus possible, and discouraged from swarming, all that such management tends to do ; but when they do swarm, they are to be hived and managed as are the old colonies. The increase belongs to the apiary, always ; and any system that gives a share of the increase to the laborer, will defeat itself and prove in the end damaging to both parties. The old system of half the honey and half the increase, and the lessee or laborer furnish everything, is illy adapted to modern apiculture, and would give the capitalist the ' lion's share.' Of course the surplus from the increase is divided equally, the same as that from the old colonies."

To be sure each individual contract or agreement, may reasonably be varied, to better suit any special conditions existing in the case. I lay down general outlines that I think if carried out, will come very near to doing justice to both parties. When we have the wintering problem under universal control, these terms could well be modified in favor of the laborer.

CHAPTER VI.

Subduing Bees.

As my experience in the matter of subduing bees, has taught me a little differently from that of those laid down in other works, perhaps I can shed a few rays of light upon the subject, after all that has been said by many better writers than myself.

A vital point in mastering bees with smoke, is to smoke them so as to frighten all the bees in the hive, before you cause any jar or do anything that shall irritate them before they have capitulated. When bees are once thoroughly aroused with anger, no amount of smoke, however applied, perfectly conquers them till they forget the cause of irritation.

I have seen whole apiaries continually irritable, in fact, dangerous to walk through without a face protector, that became so from no other cause than bad management with the smoker. The operator would either fail to smoke the colony at all, or smoke them only in part, before he would rattle a board on the hive, or tunk the cover, or roughly remove it, or make some reckless movement that put the bees on the defensive, and often the aggressive; after which the smoke would not completely conquer them. Such ignorant or careless handling, builds up a belligerent disposition in our bees that I believe becomes in-bred in them after a few generations, and then we have what we may call a strain of ugly bees. We should always be very careful to make no jar, or do anything to cause irritation, or even suspicion, upon the part of our bees till we have poured a stream of smoke upon the guards, and, unless during a heavy honey flow, into the entrance of the hive, sufficient that every bee may take affright. Then we should remove our shade-board, if we are using it at the time, and noiselessly remove the cover enough to pour a volume of smoke in at the top of the hive, when we may rattle and jar all we please thereafter, which at that stage of the operation, seems only to more completely subdue the bees.

We have been told that the reason the application of smoke puts bees in a friendly attitude, is because it frightens them, which causes them to fill themselves with honey, and when so filled, they cannot without disgorging the same, assume an attitude in which they can use their stings. While this teaching may be correct in part, I think that the effect of smoke is to frighten out of them, all ideas of battle. It seems to instantly impress them with the utter uselessness of opposing "an enemy with a breath like that."

We handle bees very rapidly and sometimes quite carelessly, outside of the period above mentioned, and we never wait for our bees to fill themselves, after they are once thoroughly frightened, which can be accomplished almost instantaneously. Of the above philosophy I think I have had ample proof.

In a few instances I have had prime swarms when hanging on a limb, act so ferocious as to make their hiving a job to be dreaded. A few blasts from the smoker has always subdued them almost as quickly and perfectly as when upon their combs, and certainly no "filling themselves with honey," is possible here.

We sometimes hear an apiarist boasting of how little smoke he can get along with. This always strikes us as an evidence of his lack of knowledge upon this subject. Where such smoke is used as described under the head of "Smokers," no harm can result therefrom; while much harm may result, or time be wasted, from not using it freely, wherever it can possibly be of any aid to the operator. I know of but one instance wherein its use can do harm, and that is in smoking the guards of a colony that is in danger of being robbed.

While very many of my readers, contrary to most of the recognized authorities, may have learned to recognize the above points, any who may not, will be highly gratified with the results they will achieve, if they in future work in accordance with them.

--- · ---

CHAPTER VII.

Increase.

I have always been an advocate of natural swarming, as the best method of increase, especially for those of limited experience with bees. My past seasons' experience, and correspondence with a friend, one of the foremost bee-keepers of the country, has convinced me of many points of superiority in artificial increase, and I have engaged him to write a portion of this chapter, feeling that his broad practical knowledge eminently fitted him to do so, and herewith present it with such comments as are suggested by my own experience:

"To the practical bee-keeper, whether he numbers his colonies by the tens or hundreds, the increase of his stock is a subject of more than ordinary interest and importance. While our success in applied apiculture will materially depend upon our methods of management in its various departments, and the energy and skill which directs them, this question of increase we deem to be an important factor in the problem of success. That, increase of stock, more or less rapid, is conducive to the best attainable results in honey production, is, I believe, conceded by our best, practical apiarists. Such has certainly proven true of my experience in bee-management. The increase of all types of animal life is a universal law of nature, which is the basis of whatever degree of success may be attained in our own pursuit. Yet, a blind adherence to nature will often militate against us. The reason of this is apparent when we consider that nature in her varied and marvellous manifestations—embracing the universe—takes no thought of, and cares nothing for the special success of any of her many forms of life. While nature should be our guide in so far as she works in our favor, beyond this point the intelligent hand of the bee-master must guide and control, for the end to be attained. It is the final results in dollars and cents, for which we are striving and with this object steadily in view, we submit such plans as our own experience has shown to conserve this result.

While we have in the past regarded natural swarming as a preferable mode of increase, under a great variety of conditions and circumstances, this method is always open to many objections. Among these we may name the time required in watching for and hiving swarms; the loss of queens by mixing of bees; absconding swarms and the time lost by the queen in laying and the bees storing honey, it being a well-known fact that the queen lays sparingly and the bees store honey with a diminished energy while preparations for swarming are in progress. As an offset to these drawbacks, it has been claimed that natural swarming imparts an added degree of energy to the bees, that is otherwise unattainable—a claim which I am at present more than inclined to doubt. But to those, who for any reason, prefer natural swarms and a moderate increase of stock, with the best results in surplus honey, either comb or extracted, we suggest the following:

Hive your first or prime swarms upon full sheets of wired-foundation (if you have no empty combs), in a new hive placed upon the old stand, removing the old colony to a new location. This removal will materially add to the working force of the new colony and prevent the issue of second, or after-swarms from the old one. The work of hiving natural swarms may be greatly facilitated by shaking a few bees (from one-half to one pound) upon the top of the frames, quickly replacing cover of hive, shaking balance of swarm upon a broad board placed in front of hive and upon a level with the entrance. The bees in the hive will set up the call peculiar in such cases, to which those outside will respond, and at once join their companions. Thoroughly spraying the bees with cold water, when clustered, before shaking from the tree or other clustering place, will facilitate their easy and rapid manipulation. Bees may be held upon the tree any length of time by spraying every half hour; but care should be exercised not to use too much water. We have found a ' Whitman Fountain Pump ' excellent for this purpose.

The forced increase of colonies by what has been termed 'artificial swarming'—a term that I do not like, but use for lack of a better one—has been met with many objections, some of which, I freely admit, have been shared by myself. But longer experience has convinced me that these objections arose from the faulty methods in use, and were not necessarily inseparable from the system itself. I can see no valid reason why a forced increase of stock, that shall secure the essential conditions of natural swarming and at the same time obviate the difficulties attending it, should not be adopted; provided equal or better results are thus attained. It is the returns, the net cash which an apiary can be made to yield, that we want regardless of any theorizing or our own preconceived ideas. We are ever ready to supplant the old by the new, when such a change shall be advantageous, and the two methods given below have been attended by very gratifying results, in our own apiaries for many years past:

PLAN NO. 1. From a full colony, remove two frames of brood and adhering bees, placing them in an empty hive, which we will designate as hive No. 2; the old hive from which they were taken, as No. 1. Shake adhering bees from another comb of brood from No. 1 into No. 2, replacing this last comb in No. 1. Put empty combs or frames of foundation, in place of combs of brood removed from No. 1 and move it to a new location, with its old queen. Put hive No. 2, on stand formerly occupied by No. 1, giving it a frame of empty comb on each side of its two frames of brood, contracting unoccupied space in brood chamber by ' dummies ' or ' fillers.' Now perform a like operation with your strongest colonies, say one-fourth, or more in number. Eight days later you can start nuclei as above described, from such of your remaining colonies as you wish to divide, giving them queen cells on the following day, from nuclei started nine days before. When the queens have hatched in these nuclei, we give them each an additional frame of brood, taken from the colonies retaining the old queens. This last frame of brood should be eggs and unsealed larvæ; but the two frames first used, ought to consist largely of sealed brood. Now you will discover, if you have followed us closely, that this plan is simple, readily understood and easily operated. By it we have first a nucleus upon the stand occupied by the old colony, which can itself be readily built up to a full colony—one that will give us fine returns in surplus honey. The old colony, removed to a new location, loses just enough of its working force to obviate the tendency to crowd out the queen and swarm, yet retains the vigor and force of a full working stock, giving us two hives for business, in place of one—and at a season when most desirable—during the clover harvest. We may add, that to secure this result, our first nuclei are started during fruit bloom in the spring. For the comparative value of queens reared by this method, see chapter on ' Queen Rearing.'

If bees are too weak in numbers during fruit bloom, or for any other reason no provision for increase has been made until the advent of the clover harvest, or the swarming season, we have recourse to PLAN No. 2:

Remove old queen and one frame of brood (unsealed prefered), placing same in centre of new hive, filling up on either side with frames of foundation or empty combs. Place new hive on old stand; shake two-thirds of bees from old hive in front of new one, and remove old hive to a new location. On following day, give old stock a queen cell or virgin queen just hatched; or if these are not at hand, let them rear their own queen. If you have a supply of fertile queens, introduce such immediately after division is made, as per directions for 'Introducing Queens.' When this is done, the old colony will soon be in a prosperous condition, and will store surplus rapidly during any good honey flow; while the new colony, occupying the old stand, has the old queen, a good force of working bees of all ages; in short, just the class of bees you would have had in a natural swarm, with none of the drawbacks and perils of natural swarming. In this connection we may observe that the time required to hive one natural swarm, will suffice to make three divisions as above described—quite an item when the apiarist is crowded with work in this, his busy season. Those who prefer no increase of stock, but wish to devote the whole energy of the bees to the production of honey, may in our judgment, best secure such a result, by requeening their colonies just before, or at the beginning of the honey harvest. By this plan we secure the threefold conditions, so essential to success:—young, vigorous queens, the non-developement of the swarming impulse, and the highest energy and sustained industry in honey gathering. From long-continued and carefully conducted experiments, we unhesitatingly pronounce this method incomparably superior to the use of any of the many forms of non-swarming attachments often recommended by apicultural writers.

In concluding this subject, we may add that queens reared according to directions given in the chapter on 'Queen Rearing,' show but little tendency to swarm. Especially is this the case when the hives are properly shaded from the direct rays of the sun, and abundant room for storing surplus honey be provided. In the same chapter will be found the reasons for such directions herein given for making forced increase of stock, as are not explained in connection therewith, as they are closely connected with queen rearing, and come more properly under that head."

In practicing the first plan of artificial increase laid down by "My Friend," I wish to caution you in regard to protecting the old colony against any sudden change in the weather, causing a lower temperature, for you will notice that the parent colony contains much brood, and has just lost a large force of bees. I would advise arousing the colony, smoking it thoroughly, and leaning a narrow board against the front of the hive to cause the outgoing workers (after the division) to mark their new location; thus tending to retain a larger force in the parent colony, than would otherwise remain. Italian bees will not return to the same extent as will the Germans. In inserting empty frames, or even frames of foundation, between frames of comb, it often happens that the bees take this opportunity to enlarge the adjoining combs beyond a proper thickness, thus making the new comb proportionately thin, greatly to our disadvantage. To avert this difficulty, see that the combs adjoining your frames of foundation are well brooded, which prevents farther extension of them, leaving room to build the new comb to proper thickness. Reversible frames also aid us in averting the above mentioned difficulty of inserting frames of foundation between frames of comb, at will.

The second plan of artificially increasing our colonies, given by "My Friend," has been practiced by the author to some considerable extent. I have only to suggest that one-half, rather than "two-thirds" of the bees be driven from the old colony. This amount, together with the number that will return to the old location, will balance the old and new colonies about the same as natural swarming would have done. If the colony has already taken on the swarming impulse, a greater proportion may be driven, but under ordinary circumstances, 1 must caution against driving more than an estimated one-half of the bees.

The foregoing, is supposing some increase is desired. Regarding the total prevention of swarming, I know of no sure way to prevent it. I know of no one who does. It may be greatly discouraged by always giving the colony plenty of room, and keeping the hive well shaded, and doing this before the swarming impulse pervades the colony, all of which will be described in the chapter on "Hives."

Though I have never practiced the plan of requeening early, as given above by "My Friend," it is one upon which I look with favor; more especially as it has valuable advantages independent of preventing the issuing of swarms.

Centuries have passed since it was known that the queens, drones and workers varied greatly in size. Based upon this fact, all sorts of devices have been constructed to control swarming, by preventing the escape of the queen and subjecting the workers to passages of egress and ingress too small for the queen to pass through.

I will now endeavor to describe an arrangement I invented ten or twelve years ago, and laid aside as impracticable. Why impracticable? Mainly because of the trouble with the drones, (especially in hives where they were more numerous) almost totally preventing the bees from ventilating their hives.

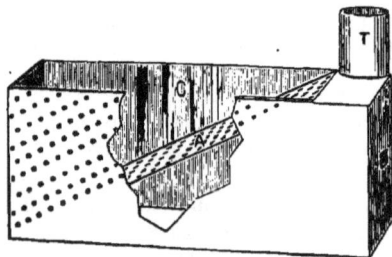

In viewing the above cut, imagine yourself looking at a tin box, 14x6x4 inches, with both sides open. (In the cut, one side is up, and the other down.) You see an angling partition A, passing from one corner of the tin box to within two inches of the other. This closes the opening through the box, except the space 2x4. This space is closed by a piece of tin 2x3⅜, and the remaining opening, 2x⅝ has a flat tube T of the same dimensions and about 2½ inches long, open at each end. The partition A, and all of that part of the box above the partition, and on the side towards you, is perforated with round holes made with a punch, with the bur projecting on the outside. The holes are made just large enough to freely pass a worker bee when empty, and as there is no necessity for laden bees to pass these holes, they can be somewhat smaller than the ordinary contracted passages, and too small to admit of the passage of one unfertile queen out of one thousand. This attachment I made when I used the ten-frame Standard Langstroth hive with portico. To adapt it to my present hive whose inside dimension across the frames is eleven and one-half inches, let us imagine it twelve inches long, instead of fourteen inches, and the left end (as you face it) also perforated. To adjust it to the hive, we lay the side C on the alighting board, shove it up tightly to the hive, pushing the tube T into the entrance and under the bottom bar of the side frame.

The perforations are thickly located; in fact, the tin is almost all holes. Now let us describe the actions of the bees, as we have watched them many an hour. A worker starts out to the field, he rushes to the entrance, looks at the new obstacle, accepts the invitation given him by the division A to pass to the right, goes down near the corner, slips through a hole, takes a look at the new order of things, sees that he is in the right church, that the pew is only newly ornamented, and strikes out for the field. Another, and another, and another follow in rapid succession, all passing out near the corner, induced by the position of the angling partition A. The inner end of the tube T, being within the hive and quite dark comparatively, only about one worker in one hundred passes out through it; besides it is constantly in use, by those passing in.

By this time the " nectar-laden bees " begin to return. Of course they propose to enter at the point of exit. They look at the holes. Sometimes · stick their heads into one. The " grain " of this hole, you remember runs the wrong way, besides it is so small as to be poorly adapted to the tired and swollen-bodied, laden worker, even if passed the other way.

Once again the angling partition invites the little worker to the right, which invitation he immediately accepts, and passes through the tube T. You will readily conceive that this tube is large enough to admit of the passage of the working force of the strongest colony, because the current flows all one way. (I think we used a tapering tube, it being only about one and one-half or one and one-fourth inches wide at the inner end.) In two or three hours, the bees seemed to have perfectly learned the attachment, and accept it cheerfully, almost the entire force passing out and in at the respective places designed for egress and ingress.

I have again the past season, used the above attachment, also another made by Mr. Alley, of Massachusetts, and a new one of my own construction, embodying the " angling partition " principle, together with the cone, as used by Mr. Alley to trap drones, and the queen when the bees swarm. I cannot say that I consider any of these attachments practical, and I do not think they will ever come into general use. I may be mistaken, and give this only as my opinion, and leave this principle to be experimented with by any and all who have a desire to do so.

What is far more desirable, and I think desired, by most of my readers, is the

PREVENTION OF AFTER-SWARMS.

My name has become associated with a plan for the above purpose, which works perfectly with myself and others, and has been described in our apicultural papers, and which I quote as follows, from GLEAN-INGS, of June 15, 1885, page 414:

HEDDON'S METHOD OF PREVENTING AFTER-SWARMS.

" Several have reported success in preventing after-swarms, by simply hiving the prime swarm on the old stand, and removing the old hive to a new location. They claimed the cause of success to rest in the fact that this removal drained the old hive of a larger proportion of its bees, especially the older portion; and so when the young queens came to hatch, the bees would find themselves too few in numbers to swarm, and all super-numerary queens would be destroyed, and thus no after-swarming would take place. The theory is correct, but I found that it did not go far enough to insure success. I added to it by practicing the following:

About eight days after a colony casts a prime swarm, the queen-cells, that were left behind to requeen the old colony, begin to hatch. The first queen out instinctively scents danger from rival queens that will soon hatch from the other queen-cells; so she at once attempts to destroy her rivals by stinging them before they come out for even battle. The bees seem to dislike this act of depravity, and to postpone bloodshed they divide up, a part coming out with this queen (sometimes two or more queens) while the rest remain to await the hatching of the other cells. Thus we get after-swarms. They seem to be Jack-at-a-pinch swarms, and not the fulfillment of natural desires, as are prime swarms.

Many times several of these after-swarms are cast, and it often seems that they never would cease as long as the queen-cells hold out, and the old colony could furnish workers to make up these little swarms. We have been advised to stop this after-swarming by clipping all the queen-cells but one, soon after the prime swarm issues. This method is a good one in theory; but in practice, bee-keepers have found that too often the cell left, will fail to hatch. Oftener the bee-master fails to get all clipped but one, and out comes his second swarm when he is least expecting it.

Practical honey-producers are asking for something else, and here is the system of management that I adopted some years ago, and advocated, and one which W. Z. Hutchinson and others have tried and reported successful.

Let us suppose that colony No. 8 swarms June 15. With a non-erasive crayon we mark upon the hive, 'O, June 15,' and on the hive in which we put the swarm, 'S, June 15.' Thus we distinguish the old colony from the swarm at a glance, as we make these marks in large characters.

When we hive the swarm (always on full sheets of wired foundation), we place it on the old stand, moving the old colony a few inches to the north (our hives front east), with its entrance turned northward, away from its swarm about forty-five degrees. As soon as the new colony is well at work, having their location well marked (say two days), we turn the old colony back parallel with the new one. Now both hives face east, sitting close beside each other. While each colony now recognizes its own hive, they are, as regards all other colonies, on one and the same stand.

The dates on the back ends of the hives indicate that second swarming may be looked for about June 23. About two or three days before that date, and when the bees are well at work in the fields, we remove the old hive to a new location in another part of the apiary. This depopulates the old colony, giving the force to the new, leaving too few bees in the old one for the young 'Misses' to divide; and as they at once recognize this fact, they light it out on the line of 'the survival of the fittest.'

Remember that you are to remove the old hive to its final location, when the workers are mostly in the field, and move it carefully, so that very few old bees carried away with it will mark the new location.

It is supposable, that when the old colony swarmed it contained two or three tiers of surplus sections, more or less completed. It is well to at once place part of them on the swarm; and when the final removal of the old colony is made, the rest may also be placed there; in which case there will be no loss of surplus by robbing the old colony of so many bees—not if your hives are properly constructed, arranged and manipulated.

The old colony contains no very young brood, and very many newly hatched bees, so there will be no loss of brood by this operation—not in swarming time, in this locality and latitude.

In six to ten days the old colony will have a fertile queen, as a rule, and become quite populous, when surplus receptacles may be adjusted to it.

In my practice with this method, and the practice of many others who have used it, I am not aware of one instance of failure. The plan embraces the advantages of speed and certainty. It is done in half the time you are reading this chapter. There is no hunting for queens or queen-cells, or even opening the hives. It needs only to be properly executed to be appreciated.

If we are going to produce cheap honey at a profit, all our operations must be executed by just such simple, practical and successful methods. We must manipulate hives more and frames less. All our hives must be readily movable, and we must make everything work as nearly automatic as possible, and turn out first-class surplus honey."

I do not practice what is called "Clipping the Queen," which consists of cutting away part of one of her wings, so that when she issues with a swarm, she cannot fly, for I have found in my locality and surroundings, such clipping only complicates the troubles of natural increase, and that the bees are apt to forever be more or less jealous of the presence of a wing-clipped queen. With them, they are more apt to swarm, or super-cede them.

CHAPTER VIII.

Queen Rearing.

Of all my acquaintance, I know of no man that I believe to be as well versed in this branch of our pursuit, as " My Friend," who has at my sol-icitation, penned the following, based upon years of extensive experience in queen rearing:

" A bee is a bee, and that's all there is of it.' How often in the past have we heard this idea advanced in some form or other, while at the present time it is by no means uncommon. In support of the advanced ideas of to-day, regarding the breeding of bees, we may cite the wonderful pro-gress that has been made in the breeding of our domestic animals; the im-proved milk and butter qualities of our cows, the beauty and speed of the horse, the docility and sagacity of the dog, the fattening qualities of the hog, the prolificness of fowls, and the almost numberless other instances of progress in the same direction. Yet we are met by the same incredu-lous smile accompanying the old observation, 'Oh! yes, but a bee is only a bee.' Let us see how much of truth there may be in this hackneyed phrase. If we accompany the owner of an apiary who has paid little or no attention to this subject of breeding, we will find a yard, the bees of which, possess characteristics differing widely from each other. Here we find a stock, peaceable and industrious, close by another that is very belligerent, seem-ingly anticipating, and always ready for an attack. A third one that has made a 'two-forty' record in the line of swarming, yet others that are good comb builders and honey gatherers, having ' made their pile ' of sur-plus, while this one is weak in numbers and generally valueless, and that one always ready to rob its neighbor of its honeyed stores, or follow the apiarist about, with a tenacity and venom that makes life (in a bee-yard) miserable. And shall we say in this age of rapid progress and wonder-ful achievements, that the apiarist can do nothing to remedy such a state of affairs? That while his brothers in other pursuits are steadily sur-mounting the obstacles that lie in their pathway, he is powerless to un-lock the secrets of nature and use them to his own advantage?· Our only answer is, that everything depends upon the apiarist. If he bring the same skill, tact and perseverance, to his work, as has been shown in other pursuits, success will crown his efforts; otherwise he must remain con-tent with the same heterogeneous traits of apis melifica, already enumerated. Granting that a better condition of affairs is alike devisable and obtainable, what is the royal highway that will bear us to the long sought goal?

Briefly stated, we may say that the law of evolution, as applied to species, is the basis of the superstructure which we wish to build. Discrimination in selection and careful breeding, will give results that will amply recompense us for the time and expense necessary for the elimiation of undesirable traits, and the attainment of those characteristics which are now so generally conceded to be especially desirable. The first step is the selection of queens for breeding. For this purpose, choose such as have proven prolific, keeping the brood chamber well and compactly filled, under adverse, as well as favorable conditions, and whose worker progeny are hardy, peaceable and industrious, adhere well to the combs in handling, defend themselves against enemies, are good comb-builders and not only maintain, but show a marked tendency for improvement of these qualities in their queen progeny. Those who have had large and extended experience in queen-rearing, can appreciate the importance of this last mentioned tendency. And just here we would say, that we consider the selection of drones for fertilization, as an important factor in the successful solution of this problem. They too, should be reared from such stocks as show in the highest degree, those traits which we wish to establish. Having selected our breeding stock, the measure of success that shall attend our efforts, will materially depend upon the skill by which they are directed, inasmuch as the methods employed must radically affect the final results. We are often reminded that nature must be our guide, if we would achieve success in this branch of apiculture. In some measure this is true, and yet nature is often faulty in her processes; defeating the cherished result we are earnestly striving to gain. Having long appreciated the importance of this fact, as applied to the subject in hand, we submit our favorite method of rearing queens—one which has given us the most uniform and satisfactory results.

Before doing this, however, we wish to say just a word relative to the existing prejudice against what has been termed 'forced queens.' Many years ago, that close observer and able writer, the late M. Quimby, wrote an excellent article upon this same subject, in which, after detailing his methods and recommending a little box and a handful of bees for the purpose, asks this question—'Have I made it plain now, that brood and nurses can be economically adjusted?' We quote the above to show that Mr. Quimby, although an eminent practical apiarist, made the same mistake, so often committed by others, in supposing that because a small quantity of bees can construct queen-cells, that they are capable of doing the work as well as bees that are in a normal condition. In the light, not only of our own past experience, but that of many others as well, we would broadly state as a rule, whose exceptions are exceedingly rare, that fully developed queens cannot be reared by bees so situated as to be in a sluggish, abnormal condition. If we desire success, this condition must be avoided, and here is our way of doing it:

From your breeding stock, select a comb of just hatching larvæ, placing it in the center of an empty hive; upon either side of this comb, put two combs partially filled with honey, and if they contain some pollen, so much the better. Your hive will now contain five combs, four of honey and pollen, and one of larvæ. Outside of these combs, place a 'dummy' or 'filler,' as a protection against extremes of temperature. Now we place this hive for queen-rearing, upon the stand of some strong colony, brushing off the bees from two or three combs, into it, and removing said colony to a new location. This gives an abundant working force of bees, of all ages, in the same location to which they have been accustomed, and being deprived of their queen, will immediately proceed to the rearing of the queen-cells to supply her loss. Twelve days afterwards, these cells will begin to hatch and the young queens can then be given to strong nuclei, where they are to remain until fertilized and laying. To secure larvæ of uniform age, insert a frame of worker comb in your breeding stock or stocks, four days before you wish to start cells. The number and location of queen-cells may be partially determined in advance, by simply breaking down with the point of a knife, the lower partition of a cell containing the larvæ you wish developed, and the two cells immediately beneath it. The months of May, June, July and August, are the most favorable for queen-rearing in this locality, and to secure best results, cells should be started during a good, or moderately good, honey flow. We may add, that giving the bees a comb of eggs and larvæ, ten days after cells are started, is highly advantageous. The modus operandi of this method is simple, producing the very choicest of queens—vigorous and finely developed. They may be allowed to hatch and then run in at the entrance of a nucleus or full colony, that has been queenless twenty-four hours, smoking the bees moderately at the same time. Queens reared by this method, while equal in point of vigor and every other desirable characteristic to any reared naturally under the ' swarming impulse,' differ widely from this latter class in one important feature, viz.:—in being disinclined to lead out natural swarms. From close observation and a somewhat extended experience with queens reared by this method, I fully believe that the swarming instinct may be practically bred out of our bees, and at the same time perfect their other desirable qualities. This we deem to be an important feature, facilitating and simplifying the labor of the apiarist during the busy season, enabling him to secure far better results in honey production, with less labor, worry and general friction."

In my opinion the above generalities given by " My Friend," embrace some of the grandest truths upon which successful apiculture is based. Especially is this true of what he says regarding the possibilities of improving our stock. I have never been so fully impressed with this great truth, as now, after again going through a campaign with two hundred colonies of bees (spring count) one-half of which were purchased of four different apiarists.

Before giving you a detailed outline of our preferred method of queen-rearing, one which we are now practicing with very satisfactory success I wish to again call your attention to the important truth, that in apiculture as well as other lines of culture, art, if properly applied, may excel nature. I believe we get better queens and more of them, by the following process, than nature gives us through her system of natural swarming. Once I could hardly be made to believe this, but experience has forced me to recognize the fact.

We proceed to rear queens as follows :

First, we select the colony we wish to rear from. Its bees must have proven themselves to be excellent honey gatherers, good comb-builders, and well-behaved; adhering well to their combs when handled. Their queen must never be less than one year old, and such a queen, producing bees as described, is a " tested queen," with us. When we are ready to begin operations, we select one or two new empty combs, and insert them near the center of the brood-nest of our selected colony. On the fourth day after this insertion, we examine them, and almost without exception we find them containing eggs, and just hatching larvæ. (If not, we leave them until we do.) We now remove them, filling their place with other combs. We now look these two combs over, and wherever we find larvæ just hatched, we break down the partitions between the cells containing them and those just below, as described, by putting the point of a large blade into the chosen cell, about one-fourth of an inch, and pressing downward as we withdraw it. We usually select ten or twenty such cells on each comb, and then insert these two combs in a colony prepared as follows :

Select a colony of average strength, with bees of all ages, in average normal quantities, and deprive them of their queen and all their brood, both of which may be profitably placed in other colonies, as a rule. If these bees are German or part German, they are just so much better as queen-rearers. If there is little or no honey flow, contract the hive to five L combs, or one section of our new hive. If the former, put in the fillers· Put in two combs of eggs in the center, and a comb containing some honey and bee-bread on each side of them, and fill up with empty combs. If there is a honey flow, fill the whole L hive with combs, or use a second section, or super, on my new hive. Close the hive, and queen-cell building will at once begin. Twenty-four hours later you may open the hive, and break down some more cells, where the eggs have hatched since you was last there. On the following day, you may repeat cell breaking, and you will get from forty to seventy-five large, perfect queen-cells, built by this colony. The first of these cells may be expected to hatch sixteen days after the queen laid the eggs in the combs, or twelve days after you placed them with the cell-building colony. About two days before this, and after all the cells are capped, we remove these two combs to the lamp nursery, in which we place them, keeping the temperature therein at eighty-five to ninety degrees, Fahrenheit.

For the benefit of those who may never have seen the lamp nursery, I will say that it consists of an open top tin box, double all around, including the bottom, and the one and one-half inch space is filled with water. It has a rabbet at the top, and is of the interior size of the ten-frame L. hive. It is made by Mr. Root, of Medina, Ohio, and costs, including lamp and thermometer, five dollars. We place it on an open top box, made to fit it, and place the lamp below it, adjusting the blaze, until the proper temperature in the nursery is reached, then insert the two combs, when it is covered with a board or carpet. We use the nursery in our apiary cellar, and when the proper nursery temperature is once reached, we are thus enabled to hold it within one degree all the twenty-four hours, day after day and week after week. Many would think that the proper temperature to keep, would be that kept in a colony while rearing and hatching queens. Careful observation and experimenting has taught us that there is a great variation of the temperature in queen-rearing colonies, varying with different colonies, and at different times of day and in different seasons, and that the average of all these variations is too high a temperature to keep in the nursery to have the queens come out with the most vigor. For this reason and from comparison, we believe the lamp nursery superior to any hive in which to hatch capped queen-cells. We have never seen coming from any hive from natural swarming, so many in number, or such uniformly large and vigorous queens, each one looking precisely like the others, as we bring forth from the lamp nursery and method of rearing, above presented. A perfect honey dearth is something we never have here, late years during the time of queen-rearing, since our bees work so much on red clover, and the pleurisy, spoken of under the head of "Honey Plants." But had we such dearth, we should practice stimulative feeding upon the cell-building colony. We will now proceed to outline our preferred method of

FORMING NUCLEI

in which to place these queens for further development and fecundation.

It is only necessary to form a small colony of bees with comb and brood in proportion, in which to place these queens, as fast as they hatch from the nursery, where they may spend a few days exercising for development, then fly out to meet the drones, returning to the hives fertile queens, beginning to lay in a day or two, when they may be removed to hives where needed, or placed in mailing cages and shipped to customers.

Our plan which we have practiced all the season, with uniform success, is so simple that we have smiled upon reading many laborious, complicated methods, laid down in some of our bee periodicals.

It is always about swarming time when we begin queen-rearing, and we form our nuclei, as follows :

We select one of our strongest and best brooded colonies, dividing it as described by " My Friend," under head of " Increase," plan No. 2, deviating only in so much as we place only about one-third of the bees with the old queen on the old stand. This leaves us two-thirds of the bees, and seven frames of brood, with which to form nuclei. These may be divided into at least four good nucleus colonies, by placing two frames of brood, (one extra frame of brood may be taken from any other colony that can spare it) and two empty combs in each of four hives, dividing the bees and brood as nearly equal as possible, between them, placing them in any part of the apiary you may choose. (It is better to remove them some little distance from the parent stock.)

Many will now inqure what is to prevent them from deserting our nuclei, and returning to the old stand? We place a filler just outside of our fourth empty comb, and block the entrance down to the passage of four or five bees. We place our two combs of brood between the two empty combs—all four combs occupying the regular space between one side of hive and filler. We smoke and arouse the bees thoroughly when removed, and lean a narrow board up against the front end of the hive, that the bees must fly out around, in making their exit. This causes them to mark the new location, and return to it, to a great extent.

You will remember that one-half of our bees may leave each nucleus and yet leave as many bees with the brood as are usually left in cases of natural swarming, and fully as many as are needed to take care of the brood and form a suitable home for our young queens. In our experience we have in many instances, retained too many bees, in which case we have shaken part of them back with the colony on the old stand.

Should this colony previously have decided to swarm, nearly all the bees would remain with your nuclei.

I am aware that the experiences of different apiarists, in different locations, differ. The above precautions are all that we ever find necessary here. Should you not find them sufficient in your practice, I believe that the following additional precautions will guarantee success with any bees, anywhere, and they are practical, speedy and simple :

When you first remove the newly formed nuclei to their stands, instead of giving them their liberty, completely close the entrance to their hives with wire screen. Do not at that time insert the filler, but give them full liberty of the whole brood-chamber, and in addition, a surplus case or extracting super, above—which will give them plenty of air while confined to the hive, which should be shaded from the sun's rays.

Form these nuclei in the forenoon, keeping them confined until about sundown, or just as your other bees are ceasing to fly. Now drum on the hive and smoke in the entrance a few minutes, after which remove the screen at the entrance, letting your confined bees have a flight, when they nearly all mark their new location, remaining at the same, if these, in addition to the other precautions, are used.

OUR METHOD OF INTRODUCING

these virgin queens, as fast as they hatch in the nursery, is as follows: Watch the nursery closely, so that the queens will not get old enough to kill each other, or bite open the unhatched cells and destroy the inmates. We go to ours and examine for hatched queens, about five times per day, going as early and late as we are up, so as to make the interval during the night, between examinations, as short as possible. We have not as yet, had a queen destroyed. When you find one or more hatched, place each in a wire cloth cage, and carry her to one of your previously formed nuclei; smoke the guards, and removing the stopper from the cage, place the open end at the entrance of the nucleus, and let her run in. Just as she passes in, send a light puff of smoke after her, and leave the hive with your empty cage. I think that the less you arouse the colony, the surer you are of success. I advise the use of no more smoke than to make sure of subduing the guards.

There has been some discussion regarding the best age of the nucleus, at the time the young queen is run in. Some consider such introducing safe, only after the nuclei have their queen-cells capped, which will be from three to six days after they are formed, but I have always endeavored to get a young queen in, sometime between twenty-four and forty-eight hours after formation. I have in many instances failed to have my queens on hand as soon as I intended, and have this season run queens into nuclei of all ages, from six hours to as many days, and I think not a single failure has beset our efforts. We have found about one in fifteen of our nuclei, queenless, but as we seldom look after these matters previous to a week after introducing, and have in no case found queen-cells on the combs, I infer that these queens were accepted, but were lost on their mating trip or otherwise, afterwards.

I wish to caution the less experienced, against opening a hive " to see how the queen is coming on," or for any other purpose, if it can well be avoided, within six or seven days after the introduction of any queen. I have received many letters from my customers, like this :

" I received your queen, apparently all right. I introduced her safely, and found eggs the next day after liberating, but now I cannot find her, and queen-cells are started."

Bees seem to receive a new queen on probation for the first three or four days, and if during the time, they are subjected to any disturbance, they suspect the strange queen as the cause, and at once destroy her. I have had colonies kill their old mother, upon having their hives opened. This always took place in spring.

If for any reason it becomes necessary to open a hive, soon after introducing a queen to its colony, by use of the big volume of smoke, described under the head of " Bee Smokers," be sure that you subdue this colony most thoroughly.

In introducing fertile queens, I have adopted the caging plan, and that of besmearing the new queen with honey, and dropping her into the hive at once, upon the removal of the old queen, and with both methods have very seldom lost a queen; but what may be a better and surer method of introduction, is one practiced by "My Friend," who gives it in his own words, as follows:

"While absolute, unvarying success is unattainable, as a rule, our American bee-keepers have sought some method of introducing laying queens, that would always insure success. Many plans have been proposed, which in practice, have given a greater or less degree of satisfaction. Still, the percentage of failures, has I believe, been sufficient to give the operator a thorough feeling of apprehension, whenever introducing a valuable queen to a colony of bees. After trying the caging plan, confining the queen from two to four, or even more days, resulting in many cases in the loss of costly queens, I became convinced that some method of immediate introduction was essential to complete success. I at once began to experiment with this end in view, and hit upon a method with which we have not had even a single failure, although largely practiced for the past ten years. Here is the way we do it:

Remove the queen from the colony to which you wish to introduce, then thoroughly spray the bees and combs, and new queen, with sweetened water, scented with peppermint. Let the queen crawl in with the bees, close the hive, and the work is done. We make this scented mixture, by adding half a pound of powdered or granulated sugar to a quart of cold water, and a half teaspoon of essence of peppermint, thoroughly stirring together before using. Apply by sprinkling with a small brush broom. With a particularly choice or valuable queen, we usually divide a colony as per plan No. 2, given under head of 'Increase;' spray our queen and the bees in the old colony that has been removed to a new location, and let the queen run in as before. In this case there are no returning bees from the fields, that were not scented, while the strength of the colony has been reduced just enough to give the queen a proper chance to recover from her journey (if she has been obtained from some dealer at a distance) and resume her accustomed 'gait,' at laying. I am satisfied that many fine, prolific queens are superceded by very strong stocks, on account of laying sparingly the first few days after their introduction.

The philosophy of the success of this plan, is that the colony does not realize it has been queenless, for it has not; it is simply an exchange of queens, so performed that the bees do not recognize the transaction. To absolute safety, we add the advantage of immedaite liberty to the introduced queen, and resumption of her labors, which is especially desirable in case of imported queens, or those having come long distances. We have always introduced our imported queens in this manner, with the same uniform success. This spraying method has been used and recommended by several of our best apiarists, and I only lay special stress upon the application of the principle as above delineated, because of its perfect success in my own apiary."

CHAPTER IX.

Italianizing.

The changing of black or native bees to the Italians, is called Italianizing. This is accomplished by simply removing the old queen and introducing an Italian in her place; directions for which are given under head of "Introducing Queens." If you have not a supply of laying queens for this purpose, just hatched virgin queens, as a rule, may safely be run in at the entrance of any colony whose queen has been removed twenty-four hours before, if bees are gathering honey at the time. Colonies that have cast prime swarms, will invariably accept such virgin queens any time from an hour to four days afterward, and thus prevent the issue of all after-swarms. In this way, black bees in box hives, that have swarmed, may be easily Italianized. Full and explicit directions for obtaining these virgin queens, may be found under the head of "Queen Rearing."

CHAPTER X.

Transferring.

As I cannot advise the practice, I will not describe the old method of transferring bees, by opening the hives, cutting out the combs full of brood and honey, and covered with bees, cutting them in pieces to fill, or partially fill different shapes of frames, tying them into the same, and finally ending with a very imperfect job compared with that given us by the new method, which has been published in some of the papers and given the name of

MODERN TRANSFERRING,

which I believe has been credited by common consent to the author.

I will now tell you how I accomplish this perfect change of a colony, from one hive to another, by quoting from my article on page 562 of GLEANINGS, for 1885:

About swarming time I take one of my Langstroth hives, containing eight Given pressed wired frames of foundation, and, with smoker in hand, I approach the hive to be transferred. First, I drive the old queen and a majority of the bees into my hiving-box. I then remove the old hive a few feet backward, reversing the entrance, placing the new one in its place, and run in the forced swarm. In two days I find eight new straight combs with every cell worker, and containing a good start of brood. Twenty-one days after the transfer I drive the old hive clean of all its bees, uniting them with the former drive, and put on the boxes if they are not already on. If there is any nectar in the flowers, this colony will show you comb honey. I run them together as I would one colony in two parts. Now to the old beeless hive. Of course, there is no brood left, unless a little drone-brood, and we have before us some combs for wax, for more foundation, and some first-class kindling-wood.

If you have no method by which you can use a hive full of frames of full sheets of foundation, running a prime swarm onto them at once, by all means procure it without delay. But if any one has a mania for cutting up combs and fitting them into frames, the method given above does not prohibit them from using all the straight worker-combs the old hive contains, after first extracting the honey from them. Should any one wish to increase his colonies at the same time he transfers, only the following deviations from the above are necessary: Run the second drive into another hive of full frames of foundation, and use the old hive as before. Now that we have foundation perfected, so that the bees will draw the lines or side walls to full breeding depth, in from two to three days, why fuss with the old comb from the old hive? Having once experienced the advantages to be attained by using the above method, I shall certainly never go back to the old one. All of you know what a nuisance a few odd-sized hives are in the apiary; also some who have just started, wish they had adopted some other style of hive. The above method of transferring will get all such out of their trouble.

The cost of foundation and new hives is fully made up by the better combs, and you have the change to better style of hive thrown into the bargain. I have thoroughly tested the results of the plan herein described, and am speaking from experience.

We have just practiced the above upon seventy-two colonies, and without a failure or mishap of any sort. I purchased sixteen colonies of bees; that is, I purchased the bees, brood and honey, with the agreement that I should return the hives and empty combs, which I have done. We made each one cover two sets of combs in two brood-chambers, with two queens, besides the surplus sets used above for extracting, and all are rousing strong. When you plan to double your colonies, you remove the old colony to an entirely new location, when you make the first drive. It is now my opinion, that, even without the use of comb foundation, in the days when we had none, this plan of transferring would have been the preferable one. As we are cutting out the old comb for wax, we transfer any that we find, that are perfect, now that they are all clear from bees, and brood, after first extracting all the honey from them."

CHAPTER XI.

Fertile Workers.

" It sometimes occurs, that a colony of bees becomes hopelessly queenless. By this we mean that they not only do not possess a queen, but have neither eggs nor larvæ from which to rear one. When this state of affairs obtains, fertile workers usually make their appearance, to the great annoyance of the apiarist. I have never been able to distinguish these bees from the ordinary workers. Unlike a fertile queen, they do not lay their eggs compactly in the combs, but scatter them about promiscously, always preferring drone cells, and usually depositing from two to six eggs in a single cell. As a rule, only a small portion of the cells are occupied, although in several instances I have known a set of eight L combs to be pretty well filled with eggs, in from twenty-four to forty-eight hours, and averaging at least two eggs for every unoccupied cell contained in these combs. These eggs develope in the usual way, but if laid in worker-comb, the cells are lengthened and the capping is unusually convex, invariably producing dwarf drones. If the apiarist be vigilant and watchful, fertile workers will seldom appear; but when once established in a colony, they have proven a great annoyance, from the fact that bees seem determined to accept neither queen-cells, or fertile or virgin queens. By experimenting however, I have discovered an easy solution to this problem of quickly disposing of them. Insert one or two combs of hatching bees, in the colony. Two days thereafter give them a frame of eggs and larvæ, and on the following day, queen-cells, or a fertile or even a virgin queen may be introduced, as per directions elsewhere given for introducing queens. This plan is simple, requires little time and has given us uniform and complete success, as the young hatching bees invariably dispose of all fertile workers."

" My Friend's " assurance of so easy a method of disposing of fertile-workers, was quite unlooked for, and is a happy surprise to me. He informs me that it has never failed with him, and I hope that it is one of the rules that is not confined to any one special location, but will give us the comfort and satisfaction that he has received from it.

(My former method of disposing of these egg-laying workers, has been to drum on their hive, and smoke them, until they were all well filled with honey, then place some new or weak colony, with brood and fertile queen in their place, carrying them away to the woods, or some field, twenty or forty rods from the apiary, and brushing the bees clean from the hive and combs, and scattering them as I brushed, when they would rise and return to the old stand, enter the new hive thereon, and all would go well, when I would give their combs to some strong colony to take care of. With this method I have never met a failure or mishap, and I have always practiced it, in the few cases I have had.) However, I should much prefer the new method, and next season shall test it as far as these peculiar cases furnish opportunity, trusting that I may meet with the same success as has " My Friend."

CHAPTER XII.

Feeding.

"The practice of feeding bees to stimulate the rearing of brood, is one, in my opinion, of very doubtful policy. I am aware that it is very often urged that the feeding of bees in early spring, during any period of honey dearth in the summer, or late in the autumn, to promote breeding, and thereby secure increase of numbers in the colony, will materially enhance the prosperity of the bees, and add to the income of the owner. I believe this theory is based upon a false premise. Years ago I tested it fully and faithfully, and found in every instance that I had " had my labor for my pains." I am unable to speak for those who advocate—and I suppose practice—natural swarming and the rearing of queens under the swarming impulse, or that other class recommending unscientific and clumsy methods of obtaining 'forced queens,' but, with queens bred as advised in 'Queen Rearing,' in this work, my own hives are kept well filled with brood every season, from April until October. Locality may, and doubtless does, have something to do with this question; and yet my own location is not a good one for honey, certainly not above, if as good as the average. If a colony is deficient in stores, and the adjacent flora yields no nectar, feeding of course must be resorted to; but even in this case, the addition of combs of sealed honey is preferable, if they are at command. It often occurs that the brood-chamber contains too much honey in early spring, thereby circumscribing the area occupied by the queen. This may be easily remedied, by drawing a broad knife-blade (a case knife will do) across the comb surface with sufficient pressure to break the capping, and the honey contained in such combs will speedily be converted into brood. This process should be commenced upon combs immediately adjoining the outside combs of brood, and if combs containing brood have much honey at the ends or in the upper part of the frames, they should be treated in like manner. Later in the season, when bees have begun to work in surplus receptacles, reversing the combs will more easily, quickly and speedily accomplish the desired result. If in autumn, bees have not enough stores for wintering, and their owner cannot supply the deficiency with sealed combs of honey, feeding again becomes necessary. Mr. Heddon's new feeder (see chapter on 'Apiarian Implements.') is a perfect success for this purpose, and, I may add, for all purposes where feeding ever becomes necessary or advisable. Good, pure, well ripened honey, or sugar syrup, make the best of winter stores. We make this latter feed by adding four pounds of good, clear hot rain water, to ten pounds of sugar, stirring constantly, until dissolved. Before removing from the fire, add an even teaspoon of tartaric acid, previously dissolved, for every ten pounds of sugar used, stirring briskly for a few moments to secure its even and thorough admixture. If the temperature of this syrup be about ninety degrees Fahrenheit, when fed, it will be speedily stored and capped over by the bees. I believe the best results are attained where the least time has been consumed, in feeding for winter stores. This feeding should never be done so late in the season as to preclude the bees flying freely for several days, after the final 'completion of storing and sealing of the food in the combs.

Another phase of this feeding problem, that has attracted some attention throughout the country, remains for our consideration. I refer to the feeding of liquid honey to be stored in sections, or in other words, the conversion of extracted, into comb honey, for market. That this can be accomplished, there remains no doubt. I have done it myself for the past four seasons, but with greatly varying results. The main question, in fact the only one with which we have to deal, is, is it profitable? Will it pay for the labor and expense involved? I will frankly say that this is a conundrum which I cannot answer. The feeding of several tons of extracted honey, furnishes no key for its solution. I have fed when it seemed as though perfect success was assured, and again, under precisely similar conditions for aught I could see, it was altogether a failure. I am at present inclined to the belief that there is a law underlying the storing of honey, which none of us have yet compassed, and until more definite knowledge regarding it and the conditions of success are obtained, I am forced to regard feeding for this purpose, unadvisable. It is barely possible that feeding to secure the completion of unfinished sections, may pay, and thus prove the exception to the rule above given."

My experience, like that of " My Friend," as given in the foregoing, is, that as far as receiving any benefits from "stimulative feeding," I don't think I should keep a bee-feeder in my apiary.

As long as a colony has plenty of stores, or we have combs of honey to give them, I prefer scarifying the caps of their honey (or what I think is better, reversing their combs) to any other system of stimulation.

Remember, that in this process of scarifying the caps over the cells of sealed honey, it must not be done to an extent disproportionate to the strength of the colony. It need not be done so as to cause the combs to drip, to any considerable extent.

In passing the blade over the caps, keep the advanced edge of the blade off the comb, merely rubbing down the caps which will be sufficient to cause the bees to remove them for repairs, which when once begun will end in converting much of the honey into brood.

"My Friend's" formula for sugar syrup for winter stores, contemplates feeding sufficiently early that the bees may have time to evaporate some of the water from the feed.

To make a syrup that will be when done, of the consistency of well ripened honey, only a scant three pounds of water should be used to every ten pounds of granulated sugar. I have never used more than one-half the amount of tartaric acid mentioned by " My Friend," but he assures me that his practical experience favors that amount.

I believe Father Quimby among his last labors, was experimenting regarding mixing acid with the winter stores of bees, as a preventive of bee diarrhoea, and was forming the opinion that it was well to use it in considerable quantity.

I think there can be no harm in using it in the quantity mentioned, and some brands of sugar need a great deal, to warrant no tendency towards re-crystalization.

While I prefer to have the winter stores capped over, I have known cases of successful wintering where hardly any of the stores were sealed. For three years I have experimented with feeding back extracted honey to complete partly finished sections, and also to produce comb-honey from extracted, using full sheets of foundation in the sections.

"My Friend" has expressed my opinions forced upon me by my experiments. I am far from advising such a practice.

To profitably produce comb-honey at the probable prices of the future, we cannot afford to do all our work twice over. We must make the bees do as much of the work as possible, using only such implements and fixtures as will accomplish the object sought, with the least care and labor on our part. We must depend more upon the qualities of our bees, practical adaptability of our implements, skill of manipulation and excellence of our honey field.

In some instances, with the weather and every thing just right, combined with a thorough knowledge of all the known laws governing the operation, "Feeding Back" to complete unfinished sections, might be advisable; yet it will generally be found best to extract such as are not finished sufficiently fit for market, carefully preserving the combs to be used during the most copious honey flow, of the following season. It certainly is best for most honey producers, to leave, this question to be settled by those who are best able, and most suitably situated to experiment, for this is, apparently, one of the knottiest of all the unsolved apicultural problems.

CHAPTER XIII.

Robbing.

"Among the annoyances experienced by the apiarist, in the practical management of bees, this one of robbing, often plays an important part; especially is this true where Italian and black colonies, and crosses between them, are kept in large numbers, in the same yard; and if kept in adjoining locations, this difficulty is greatly intensified. The observance of a few simple rules, will I feel sure, largely mitigate this annoyance, or prevent it altogether. The oft-repeated injunction to 'keep all stocks strong in numbers,' is a good one, yet of still greater importance is it, in this respect, never to allow your colonies to long remain in a queenless condition. A small colony of bees, normally conditioned—that is, having a queen, sufficient stores and brood in all stages of developement—is far less liable to be interviewed by the omnipresent robber, than one of four times its working force that is hopelessly queenless. Again, the entrances of all hives, should be sized to correspond with the working force it contains; especially during a moderate yield of nectar, and still more especially, immediately following the cessation of a good honey flow, like the basswood harvest, where gathering is often suddenly checked. The manipulation of extracted combs that contained basswood honey, especially, at such times, requires the greatest degree of caution. The same holds equally true of extracted combs of the previous season, that are again brought into use for the first time. In this, as in many other of the practical affairs of life, a small amount of prevention, is of more value than a large quantity of cure, however potent the remedy may be.

Only those apiarists can appreciate the full force of this suggestion, who, through accident or other cause, have had this robbing propensity thoroughly aroused, and experienced the pandemonium state of affairs that ensued. Surely, then came the time when all was not 'quiet upon the Potomac,' but rather, it was the ' terrors of the wilderness.'

If from any cause, bees have been allowed to get into a despondent condition through queenlessness, their courage may be at once revived by the addition of a comb or two of brood. While these combs should contain brood in all stages of developement, it is important that the major portion should be hatching bees, or approximating that stage as nearly as possible.

When the robbing of a colony has fairly begun, contract the entrance to a single bee passage, and a few gentle raps upon the hive will often arouse them to an effectual resistance. If however the besieged bees have capitulated, close the entrance altogether, and remove the hive to some cool place. After dark, give them a new location in the apiary, smoking thoroughly, and the trouble is ended. It sometimes occurs that bees in a normal condition, will permit a moderate amount of robbing to go quietly on, apparently unnoticed. Contract the entrance to such colonies, smoke thoroughly at nightfall, and the would-be robbers will meet with a surprisingly warm reception on the following morning."

" My Friend's " injunction to exercise the greatest care, not to let robbers get the first taste of ill-gotten gains, cannot be too carefully heeded. Nearly the whole problem hinges upon this point. In my own experience, I have not found the brown German bees, nor their crosses with Italians, any more, if as much inclined to rob, as pure Italians; but it is true that the smaller black German strain of bees, are by far, the most inclined to robbing.

I have found it true that bees will make more desperate and successful attacks upon colonies outside of their own apiary. I presume the cause for this, is that when they go long distances to rob, they establish a line of flight that is of sufficient length to at once attract bees from other colonies, until in many cases, nearly a whole apiary will join in robbing out another. Where robbing has occurred in my own apiary, I have noticed that the colony of defence is usually located some considerable distance from the one of attack.

" My Friend's " practice of placing the robbed colony on a new stand, after removing it from the cellar, struck me as a dangerous one, fearing that many bees might be lost by returning to the old location; but he informs me that in no case in his experience, has he ever known the bees to so desert, and he thinks the reason they do not, is because of the excitement caused by the robbing, and the presence of robbers in the hive, which after their confinement, mostly remain and strengthen the colony. When I had ascertained that only one colony was doing most of the robbing of another, and just which one it was, I have stopped the nefarious business at once, by changing stands with them. You will see what surprise and confusion must occur. After all, the best cure, is prevention.

CHAPTER XIV.

Bee-Enemies.

" Under this head I propose to group a few thoughts upon the diseases and enemies of bees, that seem to be of particular interest to the specialist. The bee-moth that cut so important a figure many years ago, in the destruction of brood-combs, both occupied and unoccupied by bees, has, by the introduction of movable frames and Italian bees, been stripped of its terrors. Still it is an ever present enemy, and requires watchful care on the part of the bee-keeper. Even with movable frames that admit of easy inspection, they still infest the domain of black bees, causing more or less damage. I have never been able to carry a single colony of these bees through the working season, without the presence of the moth-worm in their brood-combs, doing considerable damage to the sealed brood, no matter how strong in numbers they might be. Upon the other hand, the Italians are almost perfectly moth-proof. I have known queenless colonies that were reduced to a mere handful in numbers, by the natural causes of depletion, to keep their combs entirely free from worms. Would we be likely to ever have such an instance of comb protection, with black bees? I deem it important to allow no refuse comb to lie around with which to breed the moth-worm. Care in this regard will reduce its depredations to the minimum.

Combs that are subjected to a temperature of twenty-two degrees below the freezing point, will remain free from worms until again occupied by bees; provided the moth-miller cannot gain access to them. Upon the other hand, brood-combs taken from the bees in warm weather, will soon be infested with worms unless kept in a very cool atmosphere, which retards their development.

The loss of bees from being caught by birds, is, I think, too small to be computed. In my own locality the law to prevent the destruction of birds is rigorously enforced, resulting in a marked increase of their numbers; yet the consumption of bees by birds, is hardly appreciable. I am inclined to the belief that they regard live bees as rather too peppery an article of food excepting, perhaps, for the purpose of seasoning their regular diet.

Where bees are kept in large numbers, (occasionally the same thing happens where the colonies do not exceed fifteen or twenty) a disease, I term ' Bee Paralysis,' sometimes makes its appearance. It affects but few colonies. Whether it would increase and spread throughout the apiary, if left unmolested, I cannot say, my experience with bee diseases having taught me that degree of caution that takes no chances of this nature. This disease affects the bees only—not the brood. The affected bees may be seen at the entrance and in front of the hive during the day; are dark and shiney in appearance, manifesting a greatly impaired vitality. The wings have a peculiar vibratory or trembling motion, and the bees have a generally sick appearance. I believe the cause to be inherent in the queen, as requeening the colony with pure Italian blood, always effectually checks the progress of the disease; and when the population of the hive consists of the progeny of the new queen, it ceases altogether. So far as my own observation extends, it is most liable to occur after a severe winter, and in colonies largely depleted in numbers, the spring previous.

I now come to a brief consideration of that most fatal and dreaded disease of bees—foul brood; and in doing this, I shall simply relate my own experience.

While passing through my apiary one day in early August, (this was many years ago) a peculiar odor from a certain hive greeted my olfactories. Upon examination, I found the colony (judging from what I had read of the disease) to be in an advanced stage of 'Foul Brood,' and a careful consultation of the then recognized authorities, fully confirmed my apprehensions. I now remembered having given another colony a frame of brood from this infected one, some eight or ten days before. 'Was that, too, diseased?' I lost no time in examining, only to find that its brood was in the same condition, but in a less advanced stage. Here, then, was a dilemma. That it was a genuine case of malignant foul brood, there was no doubt. How to get rid of the dreaded malady, was now the all important and momentous question. (I will here state that a thorough examination of the entire apiary, numbering over one hundred and fifty colonies, upon the two days succeeding its first discovery, revealed no trace of any diseased larvæ, except in the instances already given.) Mr. M. Quimby, who was the recognized American authority of his time, upon this subject, recommended the removal of all combs from diseased colonies, keeping the bees confined without food for twenty-four to thirty-six hours, when they were to be placed in clean empty hives and allowed to build new combs. If little or no honey was being gathered at the time, resort to feeding, became necessary. The honey was to be extracted, and when heated to a temperature of two hundred degrees, could be fed with impunity. All the combs of the hive were to be rendered into wax, and the hive itself thoroughly scalded, to destroy any diseased germs that might remain. In this way, Mr. Quimby assured me, the disease had been practically eradicated in his own apiary and he had no doubt of its entire success, if properly carried out by myself. Realizing the necessity of prompt action, I removed the bees from the combs of the two infected colonies, the same day Mr. Quimby's letter was received; kept them confined thirty-six hours without food, and then hived them in new hives as directed; the old hives and combs were buried beyond resurrection.

The mother of the colony in which the disease was first developed was a black queen, fertilized by a hybrid drone two years before, and was unusually prolific. When again examined, nine days afterward, more than three-fourths of the larvæ from this queen was hopelessly diseased—the other colony was badly affected also, although not to the same extent. A re-examination of the apiary at this time, disclosed the fact that eleven more colonies were also diseased, and hastening —what was to all appearances—a general ruin. Perhaps the reader may imagine something of the feelings of one, at this juncture, whose bread and butter depended largely upon honey production. for even at that time I was earning a livelihood by making a specialty of bee-culture.

Convinced of the utter futility of further experiments upon the basis already begun, I turned to the east for some light upon the perplexing problem. I had learned that Dzierzon, the great bee-master of Germany, had successfully combatted the disease in his own apiary, and believed he had obtained its complete mastery; and from the BIENEN-ZEITUNG—the German bee-journal—I learned his method of accomplishing so desirable a result. This process (somewhat modified by myself, as will. be seen by those familiar with Dzierzon's directions), was immediately put in practice, with what result, the sequel will reveal. I resolved to destroy no more bees, their combs nor hives, so long as there remained one ray of hope of saving any portion of the apiary, and if matters grew worse until 'hoping against hope,' was utterly useless, then the entire yard should be sacrificed upon one grand 'funeral pile' to appease this relentless Moloch.

The first step taken was the immediate destruction of the queens of all infected colonies. Nine days afterward, all the queen-cells were removed, and this was repeated six days later, shaking the bees from every comb, to make sure that none were overlooked. All were now hopelessly queenless. A frame of eggs and just hatching larvæ was given them, allowing each colony to rear its own queen, the object of this, being to give the bees ample time to clean up their combs, before the young queens began to lay. If any diseased larvæ remained in the cells twenty-one days after the destruction of the old queen, I carefully removed it with the head of a large pin. By this process, there was a period of about thirty-five to forty days, with no eggs being deposited in the combs, and developing no larvæ to feed the disease. Of the twenty-three colonies thus treated, the disease re-appeared in only two, and the queens of these were mated with black drones, and I am confident that some germs of the disease remained in these combs. A repetition of the above process, eradicated the last vestige of the disease from the apiary; I have never discovered one symptom of it since.

The spread of the disease was rapid; within three weeks from the discovery of the first diseased colony, twenty-two more were on the road to ruin. All these colonies contained old queens—two to three years—and all, without even one exception, were more or less tinctured with black blood—in most of the cases it preponderated. Can the reader longer marvel at my strong preference—seemingly almost a mania in the absence of this explanation—for young queens of pure Italian blood?"

It seems that "My Friend" and I differ somewhat, regarding the merits of the German versus Italian bees. I account for this upon the ground that he has never been in possession of the best strains of the former. I believe that no one can excel me, in my disgust for the little, irritable black bees. But the large brown bees, are the Germans, that possess the many valuable characteristics spoken of under the head of "Varieties of Bees." It is true that moths are tolerated by all German bees, to a greater extent than by Italians, but it is also true, at least in my experience, that all the trouble arising from their work in colonies of normal strength may be fitly compared to the depredations committed by martins, king birds, etc. Any good colony will hatch more bees in one day, than all the birds in any one locality will catch in a month. So it is with my experience with German colonies, kept in normal condition; we forget that there is any such an enemy as the bee-moth.

If bee-moths are necessary to stimulate the apiarist to keep his combs well covered with bees, then they are to the honey producer, what weeds are to the shiftless farmer, who, but for them, would never stir his soil. There are other and far more important reasons for keeping hives crowded with bees, than those connected with this moth.

Having never seen a case of foul brood, I will say but little upon the subject. I will only add, that from what I had read, I had supposed the disease was more malignant than it seems to have been in the case related in "My Friend's" experience. Such an experience must be most gratifying to him who realizes it. As is the case with robbing—"an ounce of prevention is worth a pound of cure"—yes, many pounds, and we cannot be too careful how we exchange any goods connected with the apiary, that might carry the germs.

Do not buy queens, bees, combs, or in fact, any apiarian goods, from anyone, until you have inquired into this matter. Certainly no honest man would send out the germs of foul brood, knowingly, but there is enough dishonesty and ignorance connected with our pursuit, I am sorry to say, to spread more foul brood than we care to have extant. Again, I would urge—be careful!

CHAPTER XV.

Over Stocking.

Let us first define what is meant by the term. I consider a locality, or honey area, over stocked, when it contains so many colonies, that a less number would pay a larger dividend upon the capital and labor therein invested.

I wish I could throw some light upon this obscure and important subject. I wish I knew something definite, about the most profitable number of colonies to keep in one average area, or honey field.

I had thought to confine this subject to these six words—" I don't know anything about it." I do not know as it will prove of any benefit to the reader, to dilate upon the different kinds or number of blossoms found in any given area. (By the term "area," or "honey field," we mean that area over which the bees of one apiary will usually work to advantage, which in ordinary locations, I believe consists of a nearly circular field, varying from six to eight miles in diameter, and probably containing from twenty-five to thirty thousand acres.) I presume it is of little use to tell of the number of individual bees usually contained in an average colony; of how many blossoms one bee often visits, before he becomes loaded, and returns to the hive; of how much more nectar blossoms contain at one time, than at another; of the fact that a bee cannot tell whether or not a blossom has been emptied by another, until he wastes time reaching down into the emptied nectaries. All of these, and many more points relative to this subject, have been thought of and discussed by many of our most experienced apiarists, and still they differ so widely in their conclusions, that we are left to believe that their means of gaining the much desired, and valuable knowledge, have been too imperfect to be of much practical use to their brother bee-keepers. It is a subject that has everything to do with the success or failure of the specialist; yes, and of the amateur as well, in many localities. It is one that I have been much interested in, and watched closely, for fifteen years. I have eagerly snatched and devoured all the thoughts of others that I could come in contact with, both in print and conversation, and yet I feel almost entirely in the dark regarding it.

One of the senior members of our fraternity used to believe and advocate, that no more than six to ten colonies should occupy one area. At the same time he put down the surface of that area, of a size that was so small that we know bees almost prefer going farther, to stopping within its borders; hence we feel sure that this very conservative writer, was mistaken. I will now offer seeming evidence of a little different nature, and what to me carries more weight, although it argues on both sides of the question.

You, who have carefully read reports, have noticed that by far the greatest pro rata surplus honey yields, have come from those keeping but few colonies. The same is true of their increase of stock. If I remember correctly, I have never seen one-half the pro rata yield of honey and increase reported from an apiary of forty colonies or over, that has been many times claimed for from three to fifteen colonies. Reports have been very marked in this direction. I have no doubt but that as a rule, the larger apiaries are worked the closest and best, which further points to the ease with which a location may be over stocked.

Now let us look at the other side of the question. By the rapidity with which a colony when breeding, will consume a frame of honey, weighing four or five pounds net, we think we are safe in saying that more than one hundred pounds of honey is annually consumed by a normal colony of bees (this includes winter as well as summer consumption).

In Father Langstroth's comprehensive treatise, "The Hive and Honey Bee," page 304, among other statistical records of like import, we find the following:

"East Friesland, a province of Holland, containing 1,200 square miles, maintains an average of 2,000 colonies per square mile."

If this statement, or any of the others contained on the same page are true, (they are given by the author as statistics) then it seems time wasted to talk about over stocking. According to that record, I can keep over 50,000 colonies in one apiary, and all will gather sufficient stores to be self supporting. Certainly, 10,000 to 25,000 colonies would give us a nice pro rata surplus, and an overwhelming and unheard of aggregate yield. According to another statistical report, found on the same page, I find I can keep 35,000 colonies in one apiary, and expect a nice pro rata surplus yield, for the best authorities declare that our country excels those of Europe, for the secretion of honey.

I presume that colonies differ widely, in their vigor or bravery in going long distances from the hives after honey, when it cannot be obtained nearer home. Certainly this trait can be easily bred up to a high degree of development. No doubt it has been largely developed by those who have bred for honey gathering qualities, rather than for physical markings, because it is at once one of the prime causes of honey storing success, in a colony of bees.

It costs me nearly twenty per cent. more to manage my out apiary (six miles away), than it would to work the same number of colonies in my home apiary, with those already here.

If over stocking is practically impossible, I can produce at my home apiary, all the honey I am getting from my out apiary, in addition to what I now get here, for less than one-half of the expense that it now costs me. It seems to me that no thinking apiarist can fail to see the great advantage of a thorough solution of this problem. However it may be correctly answered, there are many good reasons why it will not pay two beekeepers to work in the same area, or honey field. Breeding, robbing, etc., are all outside factors that must be taken into account, and further, it is a fact that long before a field is over stocked, according to our definition of the term, the pro rata yield begins to lessen in quantity. Besides this, honey producing in a small way cannot compete with specialty, and as there are so many rich, unoccupied fields still to be had for the taking, no two specialists should think of occupying the same field.

I am again determined to add my mite to answering the question, by continually increasing the number of my colonies, until a term of seasons, whose natural advantages and disadvantages, all considered, shall tell me something of this obscure problem.

CHAPTER XVI.

Artificial Pasturage.

Different locations throughout our country, contain so many different varieties of nectar secreting trees, shrubs, and plants, that I have deemed it best not to write a long chapter on honey plants. I could not in this little work, expect to do the subject justice, even were I competent; besides, the subject has been so well handled by Prof. Cook, Thomas G. Newman and A. I. Root, in their respective works on bee-culture, that nothing of the kind is needed, in adding another book to the bee-keepers' library. I wish however, to present a few thoughts in regard to planting for honey.

I think it may safely be laid down as a rule that it will hardly pay to occupy valuable land by planting it to anything, exclusively for honey. No doubt there are instances in certain locations, specially adapted to the plants, when the sowing of such seeds as produce otherwise valuable crops as well as honey, will pay. We might mention buckwheat and Alsike clover, as belonging to this class. However, I have most faith in the improvement of our honey field, by way of scattering broad cast, in waste places, the seeds of such honey yielding plants as combine the following otherwise good qualities:—First, tenacity. That is, they will hold the ground against weeds and grasses, increasing in numbers each year, when left entirely to themselves. Second, when their destruction becomes desirable, they can be plowed under and at once eradicated. Third, free from thorns or prickers, in other words, in no way objectionable when allowed to spread at will.

Most locations contain within the area of the bee-keepers' field, hundreds of acres of what may be termed waste ground, which is occupied year after year, by weeds, none of which are of much, if any value, and many are truly obnoxious to humanity. Certainly, he who supplants these by honey plants possessing the qualities above mentioned, not only augments his own interest, but in a broader sense is benefiting all humanity.

I know of just two plants that yield honey copiously, in my location, and which possess the qualifications before mentioned. First, pleurisy or butterfly weed, and second, Mellilot clover. I am not sure but that it would pay to occupy land of average value, suited to their growth, by sowing it exclusively to these excellent honey yielders. In the case of Mellilot clover, the land would need to be of good quality. It thrives best on gravel and prairie soils; gravel seems to be a favorite with it. If put on poor land it takes offense immediately, and in my opinion never pays for planting. Usually the plants never mature. Not so at all, with the pleurisy, it delights in poor, sandy land.

I know of many fields, so poor that they are entirely neglected, where pleurisy is rapidly taking possession of the ground. The fact that it is a perennial, is a double assurance of its successfully running out weeds and grasses. It seems to be a laughing matter for it to spring up through a sod of June grass, growing as luxuriantly as if cultivated, and slowly increasing from year to year. The seeds each have a balloon, like dandelion or thistle seeds, which insures its successful dissemination.

The plants differ widely in their period of blooming, so that notwithstanding it blossoms with basswood, it also remains to fill the gap of honey secretion between basswood and fall flowers. I noticed its first appearance about three years ago, when but few specimens could be found. Through perfect fertilization by the bees, it has so rapidly increased each year, that now we have no sudden cessation of honey flow, or robbing, after basswood. From the time it begins to bloom, bees visit it constantly, never neglecting it through the most bountiful yields from basswood or clover. As yet there is not enough of these plants in our locality to produce a surplus, and press of business has prevented us taking special pains to test the quality of the honey it furnishes. I think by another year, it will afford us a surplus. It belongs to the milkweed family, yet possesses none of its objectionable features. Bees move from blossom to blossom, as freely as when working upon white clover. I think it yields no pollen.

I have never seen a cut of this plant, and as engravings of honey plants are usually more unlike the original, than the engravings of other things, I have decided not to have one made.

For a perfect description of the plant, under the name given, I will refer you to any of the works on botany.

Descriptions and engravings of Mellilot clover, are too common to be needed here. The same may be said of the praise that justly belongs to it. I feel that I can hardly say anything too highly praiseworthy of these two plants, nor recommend them too highly, to those whose climate and soil are adapted to them.

CHAPTER XVII.

Comb, or Extracted Honey?

We often hear the question asked, which is the most profitable to produce, extracted, or comb honey? A moments reflection will tell us, "as plain as ever truth was told," that for the whole fraternity, for a term of years, there can be no difference in the amount of profit to be derived from these two classes of surplus honey production. I am of the opinion that the matter is so nearly adjusted, to-day, that each and everyone should be governed according to his knowledge of the laws of honey production, and the fitness of his climate and flora. At present, it is no doubt, best to put all dark grades of surplus honey into the extracted form. While the difference in price, between bright comb and extracted honey, is quite in favor of the former, it is just the reverse, regarding the dark grades. Dark, or amber colored honey, commands but little higher price in combs than in barrels, while the difference in price is quite in favor of bright honey in sections of combs where the producer is equipped with the requisite implements, and knowledge of how to manipulate them.

It is now generally conceded by our most experienced producers, that extracted honey, to make a good, sweet sauce, should be ripe and thick. It is furthermore agreed that, all considered, the best, as well as most economical method of accomplishing this result is to leave the honey in the combs with the bees until the cells are partly, or all sealed, or capped over. Even then, if the capping is hastily done, and the honey extracted at once, thereafter, it is liable to lose its smooth, oily consistency and fine flavor, so highly appreciated by consumers.

You will see that this method of producing extracted honey, requires almost as much time and labor upon the part of the bees, as to draw out foundation in sections, and cap it over, completely.

Considering the fact that extracted honey must compete, more or less, with syrups, butter, etc., while comb honey has really no competitor, it is not strange that it should bring more than double the price of extracted, and that the difference in price should be widening. In view of these facts, and other signs of the times, I believe it advisable, for the good of each and all of our honey producers, that all should put most of their bright honey into comb, and their dark, into the extracted form.

If our entire crop of extracted honey is to be sold in bulk, it may be truthfully said, that there is more work about running an apiary for comb, than for extracted honey ; but it is also true that such a comparatively large portion of the work connected with the best methods of comb honey production, is done indoors, and at times, when labor is worth less than one-half what it is during the rush of the season, and further, much of this indoors work can be performed by cheap, and less experienced labor, all this taken into consideration, I prefer the labor connected with the production of comb, to that of extracted honey. This is assuming that the work in both cases is to be done as it should be, and at the proper time.

Here in latitude forty-two degrees, at least two-thirds of our surplus is bright, on an average. For six years I produced extracted honey, as the bulk of my crop; then I reversed, and raised comb honey, almost exclusively, about eight years. For the past two seasons I have produced both, in nearly equal quantity and have now decided to make comb honey my main crop, hereafter.

" But," I hear someone say, " more bees will go to the fields when the combs are extracted, and no comb-builders are needed at home, hence we must get more honey when the extractor is used." Doubtless this is true, but it is equally a fact, that I can keep a greater number of colonies without over stocking my field, when devoted to comb honey storing, and without a corresponding increase of labor in caring for them ; hence I'll keep more bees, and raise the higher priced honey.

CHAPTER XVIII.

Adulteration.

Upon this subject, as upon some others, I am aware that I entertain opinions differing from those held by many of my friends—men whose intelligence commands the respect of all. I have heard them give the reasons for their opinions, and yet we widely differ.

I consider it a duty I owe the reader and one he will thank me for performing, to give my honest opinion upon this, as well as all other subjects. I believe we all agree that such arrangements should exist in society, that the truth shall be told, and all goods should be labeled just what they are.

Regarding the advantages of pure, wholesome and honest food, quite likely we do not differ, but as it is a fact that secretly mixing articles of food is a common practice in this country, and that with our commodity, honey, an exceedingly small portion of that found upon the markets is also mixed with some cheaper commodity, the question arises, "what shall we do about it?" My answer to this question is, "keep perfectly still." If this mixed article is better than the genuine, there is nothing we can conscientiously say; if it is inferior, consumers will soon discover it, and in making their purchases, will govern themselves accordingly. Thus it seems to me, there is no need for bee-keepers to agitate the question. I do not object to such agitation because of the trouble and expense arising from it, but for the reason it tends to frighten consumers, and has done so in the past, to that extent that the prevailing opinion regarding the adulteration of our product is magnified twenty-fold beyond the facts in the case.

I think our whole duty, and best policy is to take advantage of every proper occasion, when the subject is forced upon us, to inform consumers of the fact that they might have to go a long ways, and take great pains, to become possessed of a single can of adulterated honey. Of course adulterating increases the supply, but so little of it is practiced nowadays, since producers have taken small packages into the apiary, and out of the city honey houses, that as a source of supply, it does not for one moment compare with the increase in production arising from recruits in our business.

Another point is, that the city dealers, the mixers, have done much to introduce and encourage the consumption of honey.

No bee-keeper can adulterate honey with profit. If the article was a staple, like wheat, corn or potatoes, and the demand endless, adulteration might pay him for a time; but in that case he would soon drop the production of the pure article, becoming a specialist at mixing, the same as have all other adulterators.

I think consumers are now pretty well convinced that only genuine honey can be procured from producers, and the less we agitate the subject, the better for our interests.

CHAPTER XIX.

Marketing.

"If the reader has carefully observed the directions elsewhere given in this work, for securing surplus honey, and has been diligent in their practice, his efforts, aided by nature in the secretion of nectar, have doubtless been crowned with success. With this part of the bee-campaign brought to a satisfactory issue, there yet remains another problem for solution, of scarcely less importance—the conversion of this surplus crop of honey, into cash. In the good old times, when honey, stored in bulky and unsightly packages, readily sold for twenty-five to thirty cents per pound, and even at this price sought out the producer, the problem of marketing was one of easy solution; but since the philanthropic efforts to induce everybody to keep bees and secure the boundless sweets of nature, rather than let them waste their perfume on ' the desert air,' have resulted in the establishment of an apiary at every cross-roads in the country, and thereby enormously increased the production of honey—the problem is no longer so easily solved. Notwithstanding, that the poundsection of to-day, is in point of attractiveness and adaptability, to the wants of the consumer, the embodiment of perfection, compared with the package of twenty years ago, honey no longer ' sells itself.' The purchaser must now be sought, persistently and patiently, and even then our efforts are not always rewarded with success. In former times the producer named the price of his product; but that prerogative is now exercised by the purchaser. It is simply a change of position between producer and purchaser, and such has been the history of over-production in every land, in all the ages of the past.

Twenty years ago, when honey commanded thirty cents per pound, it was a luxury; to-day, when it seeks a purchaser at less than half that figure, it is a luxury still, and in the very nature of things it must forever remain a luxury. The combined efforts of all the producers and all the dealers handling it, can never change the inexorable law that makes it such. As a table-sauce, honey, in a moderate way, is a success; aside from this, it is in quantity, an utter failure. For all other purposes, it must ever compete with the products of the sugar-cane, and at a price ruinous to the producer, save, perhaps now and then an isolated locality, with unusually favorable conditions for cheap production, in very large quantities.

But the practical problem for the great mass of producers, still seeks a solution—' how can I dispose of my surplus honey?' First, we have the home market, although a small item usually, it is is nevertheless an important factor, inasmuch as the disposition of even a small portion of our products, assists in the final result. Always keeping the local demand well supplied, is advisable, as to that extent you withdraw from and relieve the commercial centers. When the wholesale markets are depressed, they will re-act against your home trade, for you cannot hope to keep the local price much above that of the metropolis.

In seeking a distant market for honey, always sell for spot cash, if possible; but as this can rarely be done, the next best thing is to consign to some reliable commission house and allow them to exercise their best judgment in its disposition. Your ' commission man ' knows infinitely more about the condition of the market and at what price your product can be disposed of, than you possibly can yourself, notwithstanding your opinion to the contrary. Speaking of reliable commission men, reminds us of the farmer, who, upon taking a grist to mill, informed the miller that as he (the farmer) was a reasonable man, all he asked was the toll; the miller might keep the grist himself. It is much the same way with commission houses. In some instances I have deemed myself fortunate in receiving even the commission. .

But the peculiarly immaculate reputation of the business is now and then relieved by an honest commission man, who will remit you the 'lion's share' of the proceeds, instead of retaining it himself. By what name this isolated specimen of the genus homo is known, in the community in which he lives, you can doubtless ascertain by repeated and liberal consignments. If your experience be of a costly nature, you can have the solace that the knowledge derived will be valuable.

In the preparation of your products for market, I take it for granted that you already realize the very great value of neat, attractive packages. At the present time when competition has become so strong, this is of prime importance. To this I may add—don't be in a hurry to ship honey to city markets. If shipped in July and August, when the market is well supplied with fresh fruits, it will not sell, in any quantity, but must necessarily lay around and become soiled and grimy, waiting for a purchaser, and thus become unsalable. About the first of October is early enough to begin shipping to northern markets. As a rule, small consignments are the safest, as you run less risk from losses by the evanescent commission man's hieing away to ' scenery new, and pastures green."

Every bee-keeper who produces more honey than his local demand will take—in fact, every specialist, begins to feel that production is in advance of demand. He notices that the old enthusiasm on the part of buyers, is dying. Many are the ways that they try to account for this unsatisfactory state of affairs. Some lay it to the practice of adulterating honey with sugar and glucose, notwithstanding the fact that liquid honey is now scarcely higher priced than sugar, and people are knowingly consuming glucose by the hundreds of barrels, in nearly every locality where commercial syrups are used. Others charge it to the use of comb foundation, forgetting that this commodity was used long before any such weakness of the honey markets took place. When our commission merchants are forced to put out weak quotations, they are in the habit of giving some reason for the low figures presented. What do these men say? Anything about adulteration, or comb foundation? Nothing. They say, " the crop is so plentiful." " California honey has come in, in car-loads."

As " My Friend " has said, " honey is a luxury," and it seems to me, ever will be, at any price at which we can afford to supply it, and as with all luxuries, it is easy to overstock the market.

What " My Friend " says of commission men, is too true of too many of them, but I am glad to be able to state that my experience with some of them has been quite satisfactory. My greatest objection to dealing through them, is the great lapse of time occurring between shipping, and receiving returns. I most heartily recommend selling out and out, for cash, wherever and whenever such sales can be consummated.

I will not speak of styles of packages, for, as which are best, depends so much upon the market upon which they are to be placed; besides, I never saw a package for extracted honey, that exactly suited me. All are too high priced, for the present price of the commodity they contain. As for comb honey, the sections and crates, described in another chapter, are the best marketing packages that I know anything about.

The reader may feel disappointed at not finding something in this chapter, relative to the styles of packages best adapted to retail markets. Also something about honey stands, for grocery stores, etc. So far, my experience with honey stands has been a failure. Different markets demand different size packages for both comb and extracted honey. In many markets, small bottles and jars, holding one and two pounds each, sell well. Since honey sells at so low a price, I have found it impossible to procure a package suitable for retailing extracted honey, the cost of which is not greatly disproportionate to the cost of its contents. I feel that it is best to leave the matter of a choice of size and style of retail packages, to each producer, who will be governed by his own peculiar local demand. Comb honey usually sells best in sections, weighing not more than one pound, nor less than one-half pound each. I find quite a little demand for the smaller size. I always expect to produce from one-fourth to one-half of my crop, in this size section.

I find that small shipping crates, sell best. They also transport more safely. I use a crate (see crates, in chapter on apiarian implements) that holds an average of twelve pounds net. I never remember of having reported but two being damaged in transit. I always ship by freight (unless in very small quantities) and consider it the safest and cheapest way.

It is bad policy to make haste to get your honey into market before others do, as it always happens that others are attempting the same thing, and a temporary "glut" results, which often weakens the market for that season. Cool weather is a great promoter of the demand for honey.

CHAPTER XX.
The Apiarian Supply Trade.

Closely connected with the success of the bee-keeper, is his relation to the trade in bee-keepers supplies. Every judicious apiarist, will see the advantage of purchasing many useful, nay, necessary implements, that he can buy of the special manufacturer, much cheaper than he can make them. It is also true that many of our honey producers can manufacture their hives and some other fixtures, at less cost than they can purchase them from far away dealers. Much depends, however, upon the local price of raw material, nearness to good accurate machinery and the skill of the bee-keeper, or his mechanic.

Bunglingly constructed implements, are not cheap at any price. Especially, is this true of hives. An illy constructed hive, either in pattern or workmanship, is forever an annoyance to both owner and inmates; many stings, that would otherwise be avoided, are among the necessary results, while manipulating them.

It is also of interest to both vendor and purchaser, that orders should not be concentrated into a short period of the season, but spread over as much time as possible. There is prevalent among honey producers, an extravagant idea regarding the profits realized by dealers in apiarian supplies. Their present profits are small, and their rapidly increasing numbers, will as rapidly decrease, in the near future. No legitimate class of dealers, can succeed better than those who support them. The time will never come when our supply trade will be a better business than honey producing, for any except those that are better adapted to it, and the same will be true of the production of honey. When honey production paid a handsome profit, so did the sale of supplies. As a dealer, I had rather have a few well-paid producers to trade with, than a host of ill-paid, and failing ones.

"My Friend," being a dealer in bee-keepers' supplies, as well as a practical honey producer, at my solicitation presents the following, upon this subject:

"In the 'good old times' (not so very old in lapse of years) of box hives, brimstone and bee-bread flavored honey, the purchase and sale of articles for the apiary was practically unknown; the apiarian supply trade was one of the things to be—in the future. But the invention and introduction of movable frame hives, stimulated the inventive genius of the apiarist and other articles and appliances of more or less value were added to our list of requisites, and presently a new phase of commercial life was · evoluted,' and · dealers in bee-keepers' supplies,' took their place in the ranks of those who carry on the world's industries. From the small beginnings of a score of years ago, this supply trade has developed into then undreamed of proportions, and a few thoughts relative thereto, may be of some value to all concerned.

It may not be out of place to observe at the outset, that bee-keepers, as a class, possess but little practical knowledge of commercial life. From the very necessities of the case—education, training and environment—their ideas are often meagre, crude and erroneous, respecting this subject. However bright and apt they may be in the pursuits in which they have been trained, they have only skirmished around the borders of the whys and wherefores of commercial life, and remembering that the major portion of the business men · fail up,' sooner or later, we readily perceive that only occasionally is one of our own ranks possessed of the natural and acquired qualifications to successfully engage in this supply trade. Tact, energy, perseverance, a due amount of caution, a thorough knowledge of the laws of trade and ample capital are all necessary to insure success.

The idea that the supply trade is the royal road to wealth, seems to have obtained with a large class of American bee-keepers., That the prices of eight or ten years ago, admitted of fair, or even handsome margins to the dealer, there can be little doubt: but the close competition of recent years, has reduced profits to the minimum. Few people not conversant with the details of this supply business, are aware of the necessary expenses incurred in advertising, postage, rent, fixtures, interest, etc., etc., to say nothing of the worry, sleepless nights and general friction resulting from unexpected mishaps and delays, and the resultant grumbling and growling of customers that cannot be satisfied.

From the foregoing, it will readily be seen, that the · cash with the order' system, becomes almost a necessity—a few bad debts would ' wipe out' the profits of many good customers. An added reason for the cash system is that the reliability and commercial standing of the great majority of apiarists, cannot be ascertained through the regular channels, while that of the dealer may usually be readily obtained through the nearest banking house.

Every straight, honest bee-keeper, who pays his debts (and we are pleased to say that the great majority are of this class) is directly interested in the cash system of payment for goods ; for, if the credit system should obtain, the margins of the dealer must be increased to cover the losses incurred by sales made to those who do not intend to pay when they make their orders, and who manifest great tenacity in carrying out their intentions. Thus, you will readily perceive that whenever you demur to this rule, established by the dealer, you insofar aid and assist that class of community who avoid the payment of their honest debts and thereby incur the application of that expressive, but just epithet—'dead beats.' The philosophy of this position we see verified in the practice of business men, everywhere; the merchant who 'trusts,' is compelled to sell at a higher figure than his neighbor who exacts the 'cash,' while in periods of great commercial depression, the former is far more likely to 'go to the wall,' than the latter. And so we say again, uphold the cash system, by paying for your goods when you buy them, thereby compelling the 'dead beat' to do likewise, instead of allowing him to obtain his goods at your own expense.

In regard to the purchasing of supplies, I would say that much depends upon circumstances. As a rule, the dealer who is properly situated respecting machinery that will do accurate work, and good material at a moderate price, can sell his goods cheaper than many can make them, while on the other hand, you may be fortunately located and save money by getting up certain lines of supplies, at home. In buying supplies, first decide upon what you need, and then buy where you can obtain thoroughly good goods, remembering that usually 'the best is the cheapest.' Bee-keepers' supplies, of fine quality and a fair price, that fully answer the intended purpose, are far more profitable and consequently more desirable than an inferior article at half the cost.

We deem this subject incomplete without still another word of advice to the purchaser. Having made your choice of dealers, make life for him as easy as possible, for you will thereby subserve your own interests. Even though you write to him every week, don't forget to always give your full postoffice address, including your county. In ordering goods, be explicit; state just what you want and how you want it. If you are writing on other subjects, make out a bill of your goods, distinct and separate from everything else. Don't mix things; don't say—' ship as before '—but plainly state how goods are to go—whether by mail, express or freight. In writing, don't refer to previous correspondence, but repeat, if necessary, what you have to say; if you compel the dealer to search his letter files, you may have to wait for an answer. Take nothing for granted: don't think that because you happen to know something in a general way regarding the person with whom you are dealing, that he knows anything about yourself, your cast-away bee-hives in the back-yard, or other exploded devices, or even of your Aunt Susan or Uncle Joshua, ' who keeps a few bees.' This writing upon the supposition that the dealer possesses personal knowledge of you, reminds us of the customer who had spent an unusual time in picking out a pair of boots, and then politely asked the dealer to have them ' charged to father.' ' Why, I don't know your father!' replied the dealer. ' You don't know him, eh? well, I know him just as easy.' In short, do business in a business like manner and you will not only merit the gratitude of the dealer, but also advance your own interests.'

The foregoing so completely covers the ground concerning troubles met by the dealer, that little more need be said on that side of the subject. I may add, that another reason why all orders should be explicit and complete within themselves, is that many dealers employ clerks, and often change them, and the incoming one knows nothing of what has been done before his arrival.

It might be well to mention the mistakes made by many in choosing their carriers. I have found that freight companies handle goods with more care than express companies, as a rule. Many make the mistake of ordering goods by express, because they do not comprehend their weight. One thousand sections 4½x4½x7 to the foot, weighs, box and all, eighty pounds, and belong to a low freight classification. Empty hives, belonging to a much higher classification, will go nearly, or quite as cheaply by express as by freight, unless they have to pass through the custody of two or more express companies, before reaching their destination. Nearly all small orders weighing less than fifteen to twenty-five pounds, had better be ordered by express, especially if they belong to a high rate of freight classification, or the purchaser is in a hurry. Many more valuable hints that might prove useful to some of our bee-keepers, could be given, but as this is a subject rarely found in a bee-book, perhaps enough has been said about it for the present. My object in touching the subject, is simply to benefit all parties concerned.

Perhaps that justice to both dealer and purchaser, requires me to add that delays in filling orders often necessarily occur; but, if actuated by no higher motive than self-interest, a reliable dealer will always fill his orders with as little delay as possible. I would also advise all purchasers to exercise a due amount of caution in patronizing dealers who recommend articles of untested and unknown value, simply to enhance their own profits, regardless of the interests of their patrons.

CHAPTER XXI.

Apiarian Implements.

In this chapter will be found a description of many of the useful implements and adjuncts of the apiary, not specially described elsewhere in this work.

As "My Friend" and myself prefer and use nearly the same devices, and his experience in the use of the same has been comprehensive, I have again solicited the aid of his pen, in their description.

"This topic covers an extensive field, and one in which the specialist is deeply interested; for, whatever of implement or device that may be brought forth, that is simple, cheap and effective, and facilitates the work of the apiarist, is valuable in a pecuniary point of view, aside from the comfort and satisfaction afforded by their use. The wants of our forefathers who kept bees in a crude, primitive way, were few and simple; but as our knowledge of bees and their management, increased and developed into a practical science, our want and necessities also increased, and in response to this demand, the genius of the fraternity has given us much that is practically useful, and doubtless still more that time and use has consigned to the museum of the impracticable and objectionable. We shall however, devote our attention to what experience has shown us to be useful, and this brings us to the consideration of the

BEE-SMOKER.

During the closing years of a useful, busy life, that veteran apiarist—the late M. Quimby, devised an implement for the rapid and thorough smoking of bees, enabling the operator to manipulate them at will. Mr. Quimby died before perfecting his invention, but Mr. T. F. Bingham, of Abronia, Mich., added the direct draft and otherwise improved the original, giving us a practical and very useful implement. In our own apiaries, the larger sizes—the ' Conqueror ' and ' Doctor '—have given us much the best satisfaction. Many different articles have been used for fuel in these smokers, more or less satisfactory to the operator, yet objectionable in some respects. The great difficulty having been to obtain a steady volume of smoke of sufficient quantity and proper quality, to promptly subdue any belligerent tendency of the bees to a contest respecting the right of the apiarist to his plan of procedure. For the past five seasons we have used pine shavings for this purpose, with almost perfect satisfaction. The only difficulty we experienced in their use, was in getting them to burn when the fire is first started in the morning, but now obviate this by first using a small quantity of punk or rotten wood (elm preferred), and when this is thoroughly lighted, fill up the smoker with shavings. Fine shavings, such as can be procured at planing mills, answer every purpose if covered with a small quantity of a coarser article, like bench shavings of carpenter shops. These last, we thoroughly dampen before using, especially if the smoker is to be run to its full capacity, as they fully prevent the issue of sparks and render the fuel more lasting and serviceable. After the fire is once thoroughly started, the shavings should be closely packed, using care not to destroy the draft or impede the free issue of smoke. A little practice will soon make you proficient in the use of this fuel, and when once used, I feel sure, will please you. Being easily obtained, lasting well when properly packed (we often use one of Bingham's 'Doctor' smokers three hours, without refilling) and producing a dense volume of cool smoke that will make even the fiercest hybrids instantly quail. Pine shavings, in my opinion, just 'take the cake' as a smoker fuel.

THE HONEY EXTRACTOR

has rendered it not only possible, but practical, to obtain a choice article of liquid honey, free from impurity and untainted with the flavor of pollen, and has added a new article to the world's commerce. Many styles of these machines are now in use, those having an inside revolving frame, with stationary cans being the most desirable. The gearing should be of the upright pattern, the revolving frame strongly made and sufficiently large to admit of receiving the combs in the same position they occupy in the hive. For supporting the combs while being extracted, we use heavy, galvanized wire-cloth, four or five meshes to the inch, drawn in toward the centre at bottom, giving it a slightly flaring position. The can should be of sufficient depth to hold four or five hundred pounds of honey beneath the revolving frame, with a molasses gate for drawing off the contents. A depth of twenty-seven inches, by thirty-two inches in diameter, is about right for the Langstroth frame. Heavy tin (2 X Charcoal Plate) or galvanized iron, will make a durable can, and it should be securely fastened so as to remain immovable while extracting combs of uneven weight. Some simple and effective device that would reverse the combs, without removing from the extractor, and without injury to them, would be an acquisition. When properly made these machines will turn easily, making little noise and throwing out the honey rapidly.

An essential concomitant of the honey extractor, is the uncapping

HONEY-KNIFE.

For ease of operation, rapid execution, and thorough, perfect work, the uncapping knife, invented and manufactured by Bingham & Heatherington, remains without an equal. In fact, it is so far superior to everything else in this line, as to merit the title of 'King of Honey-Knives.' For furnishing us with a perfect implement at a moderate price, the manufacturers have merited the gratitude of the whole fraternity.

PACKAGES FOR EXTRACTED HONEY.

Liquid honey, after being extracted from the combs, should be allowed to stand in the extractor to become clear, or drawn into tanks made for this purpose, of four to five hundred pounds capacity. From these tanks the honey may be drawn into kegs or barrels, or where smaller packages are wanted for retailing, tin cans or glass jars may be used. Pine kegs, well made and properly hooped, holding fifty and one hundred pounds, net., make as salable packages as any with which I am acquainted.

WAX EXTRACTOR.

The specialist in bee-culture will always have more or less refuse comb to convert into wax; this can be readily and neatly done, by the use of the wax extractor. This extractor consists of a small boiler for generating steam, holding a can containing a perforated tin cylinder for receiving the comb. The steam from below melts the comb, the wax running from a projecting spout into a vessel of cold water placed beside the extractor. It may be used on any cook stove. The only objection we find to these machines, is their small capacity—twenty to thirty pounds of wax being a good day's work.

COMB-FOUNDATION.

Few articles in the whole list of apiarian supplies, possess the real value for the specialist, as does this one of comb-foundation. When properly made and used, it enables us to secure uniformly straight combs in both brood and surplus apartments; facilitating their rapid manipulation; increases the value of our bees by enabling us to practically control the building of drone-comb, while it also materially increases our products, thereby lessening the cost of production. That these advantages have been abundantly proven and appreciated by the practical bee-keepers of America, is fully shown by the immense sale of the article itself. For the brood-chamber, from five to six square feet to the pound is the proper weight, while that for the surplus apartment, should run from seven to eight feet. If the base of the cell be made sufficiently thin, the presence of foundation in comb-honey will not be detected by the consumer. When used for surplus, we cut the foundation enough smaller to leave an eighth of an inch space at the ends, and one-fourth inch at the bottom, which is called filling the sections full. For fastening foundation in sections, a ' Parker Foundation Fastener ' is just the thing. In the brood frames, we use full sheets, leaving the same space at ends and bottom of frames as in sections. To prevent sagging, wire the frames with No. 30 tinned wire, pressing this wire into the foundation by hand; but this may be done more speedily and perfectly by using the ' Given Press.' There are several machines that do good work; personally, we prefer the foundation made on the ' Given Press ' and the ' Dunham ' and ' Vandervoort ' mills.

SECTIONS

for comb honey, holding from one-half pound, to two pounds each, now generally used, are an immense advance over the old clumsy, uncouth package of former years, being more attractive in appearance and better adapted to the wants of the consumer—hence are more saleable. Poplar and spruce make the finest sections, not being so easily soiled as the softer woods, and when properly made, the 'dove-tailed' section is preferable, although nailing answers every purpose. The widths in use are those known as six, seven and eight to the foot; we prefer the seven to the foot; the six being too wide and the eight too narrow. The most perfect combs are obtained by using separators, made of either tin or wood. Having tested many surplus devices, we prefer the one-story broad frame for holding these sections, as they combine the most advantages with the fewest objections.

HONEY REGISTERS

for showing the amount of honey contained in supers for extracting, or comb-honey in surplus cases, are a convenient device, enabling the apiarist to ascertain the amount of surplus of each colony at a glance. They are pasted upon the side of the super or case, having two squares of printed figures, in the centre of which a pin is driven and turned down so as to show the date when placed upon the hive or examined, and the amount of honey stored, if any, at such examination. Those devised by Mr. Heddon we deem to be the simplest and best.

QUEEN REGISTERS.

A somewhat similar device to indicate the condition of colonies or nuclei, devoted to queen-rearing, are printed and sold by A. I. Root, of

Medina, Ohio. In my own apiaries I use a small block of wood for this purpose, greatly preferring them to the register. These blocks are 2x5 inches and one-half inch in thickness. The record is kept with a lead-pencil, and when both sides are full, remove with a plane, and they are at once ready for continued service. To save time in making the record, we use the following abbreviations:

C—Cells.	V. Q—Virgin Queen.
F. Q—Fertile Queen.	L. Q—Laying Queen.
Q. R—Queen Removed	F. W—Fertile Worker.

Q 1 s—Queenless.

Thus, if we cage and ship a queen from a nucleus on July 15, we write across one end of our block—q. r. 7-15.

If we give this same nucleus a virgin queen on the following day (as is our practice), we write immediately below—v. q. 7-16.

If we make an examination eight days afterward and find eggs, we say just below the last entry—l. q. 7-24; if the queen is fertile but not yet laying, it is f. q., and if the queen has been lost in fertilization—qls.

An important advantage over the printed register is that the block of wood gives us a continuous record, which, unlike the little slate, is not obliterated by frequent rains. For material, we prefer white wood, planed smooth. Lay these blocks on nucleus cover and they are ready for use when needed.

THE LAMP NURSERY.

This very useful adjunct to queen-rearing, being fully described under the head of 'Queen-Rearing' by Mr. Heddon, anything further relative thereto is deemed unnecessary.

QUEEN CAGES.

As it is sometimes necessary to confine both fertile and unfertile queens, a supply of wire-cloth cages are convenient for that purpose. We use tinned wire-cloth sixteen meshes to the inch, cut in strips four or five inches wide, and formed around a stick one-half inch thick, by three-fourth of an inch in width and somewhat longer than your strips of wire-cloth are wide, Use a wooden stopper at each end, one of which may be securly nailed. For shipping queens by mail the cages just adopted by Mr. Heddon, are the best I have seen.

FOUNTAIN PUMP.

Where natural swarming is allowed, a 'Whitman Fountain Pump' is a necessity. By its use, swarms may be prevented from absconding, and when two or more are on the wing at the same time, they can be forced to cluster separately; and should a swarm begin to cluster in some inaccessible or inconvenient place for hiving, they may be easily driven to another location. When clustered, we thoroughly spray them with the pump, (being careful not to use too much water) which greatly facilitates the process of hiving. If, for any reason the apiarist wishes to defer hiving them, they can be held where clustered any length of time, by spraying every hour. This pump is well and durably made and with decent usage will last a life-time.

FACE PROTECTORS.

Where bees are well-bred and properly handled, little or no protection from stings is needed. In our own apiaries, we have used no protection whatever, for the past two seasons. But, where bees are belligerent, and manifest an especial proficiency in the use of their javelins, a face protector is a great comfort and convenience. A veil made of black bobinet and worn over the hat will protect the eyes and face of the operator, which seems to be a favorite target for bee venom. When bees are rightly manipulated, and still persist in stinging the hands and every unprotected place of the operator's person, they show too much 'bee-cussedness' for our nervous temperament. Thorough smoking for the time being, and re-queening, so as to weed out such blood, are our remedies.

BEE-TENT.

During a honey dearth, when bees are somewhat prone to be too inquisitive regarding the contents of each others hives, some protection against this piratical tendency becomes necessary, when colonies must be manipulated. For this purpose, resort has been had to the bee-tent, a light wooden frame covered with thin, white cloth, or mosquito-bar, and made light enough to be easily carried from place to place by the operator. This tent is placed over the colony to be manipulated, and removed after the hive has been closed. This works nicely in theory, but quite differently in practice. Aside from the necessarily cramped position of the operator and lack of room for tools, we find that when the tent has been removed, that the robbers 'pitch into' such a colony with redoubled fury, since they have all the time been anxiously waiting upon the outside for an opportunity of so doing. The one redeeming feature of its use, is the freedom afforded from stings, which are sure to be forthcoming, if robber bees have access to the hive when open. This brings us to the consideration of a device with which we may attain the object sought.

THE SCREEN-HOUSE.

We make a light frame work of strips of wood, an inch in thickness by two inches in width, of the size wanted. Personally, we prefer plenty of room, about 7x9 feet and of sufficient height to clear the head of the operator. The sides should be made separately and hooked together—likewise the cover, so as to admit of taking down and storing away, when not in use. In one corner we place a sliding door, so arranged as to slide in grooves; a slight push from either side quickly opens or shuts it. On the opposite side from the door, we place a bench, of convenient height, upon which we set full stocks or nuclei, for manipulation. Here we look up our queens, remove surplus honey, ascertain the condition of bees, etc., etc., when they are returned to their own stands in the yard, without any molestation from robbers. The cloth cover to this screen-house is made sufficiently large to hang down eight or ten inches, all around the outside of the house; by slightly raising this cover and smoking the bees, they quickly take the hint of 'not wanted,' and sail away for home without the admission of would-be robbers. Venomous indeed, must be the nature of a colony that would offer to sting the operator in this screen-house.

HONEY CRATES.

Every practical apiarist who has raised comb-honey extensively, is aware of the value of a neat shipping crate in disposing of his surplus. By all odds, the best thing we have seen in this line, is the crate devised and used by Mr. Heddon. It is 8½x12 inches and four and one-fourth inches in depth—plump inside measure—holding twelve, pound sections, six to the foot; fourteen sections, seven to the foot, or sixteen sections, eight to the foot. It also holds just one-half more in number of the one-half pound sections, of these respective sizes, all fitting equally perfect. These crates are glassed at each end in such a way as to protect the glass and show the honey to the best advantage. It also secures the great desideratum of a uniform package, for all these variations in the standard sizes of sections, is made at minimum cost of labor and material, having a small glass surface, yet showing the honey perfectly: while in attractiveness of appearance—they are perfection itself and need only to be once used to be appreciated.

FEEDERS.

While bee-feeders have not been in extensive use in the past, by American apiarists, the signs of the times seem to unmistakably point in that direction at present, and were we given to prophecy, should venture the opinion that in the near future, a good feeder will be deemed an indispensable adjunct to every well regulated apiary. We believe they would have been in more general use at present, had a really good feeder—one that would fill all the requisites of such an article—been procurable. In surveying the field of invention, traversed by the bee-keeper, we find there is little practical value in the line of feeders, aside from those invented by Mr. Heddon and candor demands the admission, that even these although correct in principle, did not meet our requirements. We are happy to add, however, that Mr. Heddon's inventive genius has finally given us a perfected feeder, which will, as we believe, give perfect satisfaction, under all the varying circumstances and conditions which render their use desirable.

They may be varied in size so as to adapt them to any style of hive in use—the sample before us, just covering the top of an eight-frame Langstroth hive and is about four inches in depth. It contains a central reservoir for receiving the feed, which flows directly into feeding apartments located upon either side of this reservoir, from which the liquid food is carried below by the bees. The excellence of this feeder will be readily recognized by the practical apiarist when we state that by its use, the feed is so placed as to avoid the possibility of attracting robbers, cannot leak a drop outside the hive and cannot daub or drown bees; the apiarist in feeding does not come in contact with a single bee—hence the rapidity of operation without smoke or stings; the honey is taken from it by the bees in such a manner as to induce the filling and capping of outside combs or sections, as speedily and perfectly as those centrally located; simplicity of construction, moderate cost, durability and of the greatest possible capacity.

MISCELLANEOUS.

Almost every practical apiarist has in use, some utensil or device, peculiarly his own, enabling him to make a 'short cut' in management or manipulation—and consequently valuable to that extent. We find a cheap clothes-basket, lined with thin cloth, into which we shake natural swarms when clustered on trees, answers the purpose admirably. If the bees have been sufficiently sprayed with a Whitman Fountain Pump, they will lie quietly in the basket without flying at all, while being carried to their new home. A good step-ladder is also a convenience in hiving swarms. A little tool, to which we attach the euphonious name of 'Spud,' is useful in prying up covers, or in taking off supers or surplus cases that have been glued to the hive, etc. Ours were made by a blacksmith from old files, are seven inches in length, an inch and a half wide at one end and flattened sharp; the other end being smaller and serving as a handle. When well tempered they make a good cold chisel, and work nicely for scraping hives, covers, etc. Other articles might be mentioned, but with such an outfit, as above described, in connection with the improved Langstroth hive, or, what is far better, where a specialty is made of honey-production, the new hive invented by Mr. Heddon, every intelligent, energetic apiarist will be enabled to succeed to his own complete satisfaction."

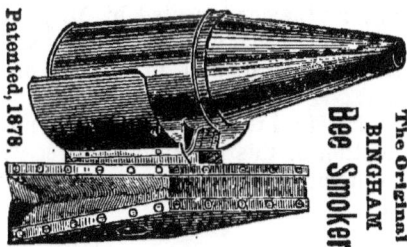

Patented, 1878. The Original BINGHAM Bee Smoker

SMOKERS.

In addition to what has been said I wish to add my evidence to the great superiority of the shaving smoke. I would not for fifty dollars be willing to exchange these shavings for any other material, with which I am acquainted, to use in our bee-smokers. With them very little heat is evolved; fully as little creosote. They settle the "cold blast" problem. Their smoke, while it most completely conquers the bees, leaves no reactionary belligerent effects with them, as does tobacco, rags and some other material. The smoke is not disagreeable to the operator No sparks fly out while using the smoke. They last a long time, when loaded into the smoker just right, a little closer detail of which I will re-present. Pine shavings, are preferable. As in most places, one can get "planer" shavings much handier than bench or hand-planed shavings, I will tell you how we have made them work equally well: First, press down to the bottom of the smoker, a thin (one-half inch) layer of hand-planed shavings, quite snugly packed. Next light some of the punk, "My Friend" speaks of, (this punk should be very light and readily combustible; only fit to start fire with) and drop it down upon the thin bed of shavings, give it a few puffs from the bellows, to get it well lighted, then fill up to near the top of the fire barrel with the pine planer shavings; pack these down moderately tight, puffing with the bellows as you pack. Now take up a small handful of the bench shavings (any wood will do for these) and douse them with water, squeeze them as dry as you can, so they will not drip, then press them into a layer about an inch deep; that will fill the fire barrel to the top. Now adjust the nozzle and puff away until the white smoke rolls forth in a volume that will subdue the worst tempered bees, whether lying outside their hive, on their combs, or hanging in a cluster upon some tree, waiting to be hived. When you notice the first spark coming from the nozzle, your smoker needs re-filling. Remove the nozzle, push these shavings (which will not be burned) to the bottom to form the bottom layer, fill with the planer shavings and cover with the dampened hand shavings as before, and you are again ready for another hour's constant use. During that time of year when no excessive or constant volume of smoke is used, one filling often lasts us five hours. No material will better hold fire than these shavings, when properly adjusted. Robber bees learn to beware of the volume of smoke that a few puffs brings forth.

With the aid of this description and a little practice, I trust you will soon be able to say with me, that "My Friend" has given the fraternity something, though seemingly small, really of great importance, to successful practice in apiculture.

For the benefit of a few of my readers who may not have seen any bee-smoker, or at least not the one invented by Mr. Bingham, I insert a a cut of the same, and will say that among the many smokers that I have tested, I count the above the best, both in principle of construction, and quality of workmansip.

I have heretofore preferred the third, of the five sizes of these smokers, but since the adoption of this new fuel, I agree with "My Friend" that the larger size is the best. I use the "Doctor," as Mr. Bingham has named this largest size.

HONEY-EXTRACTOR.

On this subject I have little to add or alter from what has been said by "My Friend." I think no extractor worthy of the specialist, has yet been given to the public. I, too, much prefer the vertical or upright gearing. Could the users of hand fanning mills be induced to adopt horizontal gearings? Further than my decided preference for the upright style of gear, I will say that all the honey-extractors offered by the different manufacturers are good, reliable machines, and do their work well, so far as I know. A choice must be made in reference to the excellence of workmanship and material used, as well as the convenience of the minor attachments. So far as I have investigated, I think I prefer the "Excelsior," manufactured by Thomas G. Newman & Son, of Chicago. The specialist, however, needs and cannot do without a machine that could not be sold for less than fifty to one hundred dollars. It should have a "slip-gearing," so that while the operator is preparing combs for extraction, a set already in the machine may be revolving by the motion given them a moment before. It should have a "foot-brake," that would stop it almost instantly. If practically possible, it should reverse the combs automatically. If not, it should be so arranged that the combs can be turned without lifting them out of the machine. It should be made of the very best of material, and with such perfect workmanship that were it a knitting machine it would take at least, one stitch. Who will give us such a honey-extractor?

The dimensions for the can, as given by "My Friend," make a very large machine; one that receives two L. frames in the position that they hang in the hive. When the screen-frames are adjusted to receive them in this horizontal position, the machine admits of a very large reservoir below, a very advantageous feature. Some theories have been advanced to prove that the honey will not readily leave the cells of the ends of these long combs when whirled in the horizontal position, but I have two of these large machines which receive the L. frames horizontally, and however true that theory may be in principle, it is never realized in practice. Our machines do their work perfectly, but they do not start and stop as easily, as our machine, with a smaller can, which receives the comb vertically. This is quite an objection to them, and the only one I think of. We always locate our machines firmly to the building they are placed in, and usually in one corner.

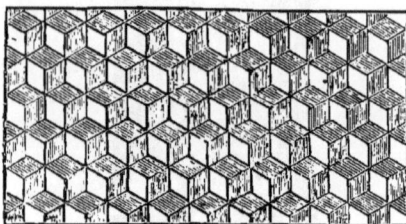

COMB FOUNDATION.

I feel that justice demands that whoever writes upon this subject, should not fail to mention the names of Charles Dadant & Son, of Hamilton, Illinois, who transform into comb foundation, more bees-wax, than any other firm in the world. Not only this, but their excellence of workmanship, added to the volume of their work, makes them at once deserving of the title of "King, Comb-Foundation." Further, I think I should commit the sin of omission, after mentioning their names, not to also mention the accuracy and integrity pervading all their business transactions with me. I have ceased to count or weigh after them, any goods they send me. I do not seek to load these men with praise, but to unload from myself years of accumulating duty and gratitude. We do not however see all matters just alike. While they prefer the foundation made upon the roller mills, my preference is decidedly in favor of that made upon the Given press. I grant that an excellent article—one that will give entire satisfaction to most consumers, can be and is made, upon any of the best styles of foundation machines, but my extended experiments, both with the manufacture and use of the article, have convinced my students and myself that the Given comb-foundation is just a little superior to any other.

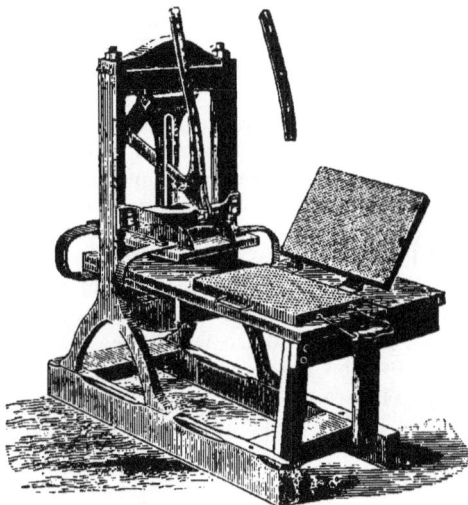

Above, is presented a cut of the Given press, invented by the late D. S. Given, of Hoopeston, Ill., and still made there by D. S. Given & Co. This machine makes a very excellent article of comb-foundation. Among the points of superiority connected with it and its product, may be enumerated the following:

1. The press is the only machine that makes foundation in wired frames.

2. It makes a sheet of wax into foundation without changing its size or shape, so that the maker can dip his sheets of the required size.

3. It makes both heavy and light foundation with no change of the machine, and both have very thin base, the wax being softly pressed into the side walls, where it is more speedily and completely drawn into comb by the bees.

4. It is very simple and easy of manipulation, and requires much less lubricating.

5. The foundation needs no paper between the sheets, to transport it safely.

Some of our leading bee-keepers have lately been enquiring as to the value of a liberal use of comb-foundation, especially in brood frames. If I am correct, their experiments are still going on, and as yet, without a definite solution of the problem. Among my many experiments, I have neglected to experiment upon this point upon a scale adequate to its solution. Mr. W. Z. Hutchinson, of Rogersville, Mich., a practical bee-keeper, fully competent to settle the question, is, I believe, still making extensive experiments, and I trust will soon be able to give us a reliable answer. I can only say, that so far as my observation and experience with thousands of pounds of foundation, goes, I am now in favor of filling completely, all my brood frames and surplus receptacles. I believe that the verdict will be, " for profit, use all the foundation you can." As to the pleasure of its use, there is no question. The fact that the use of the article saves time and honey, is not all the benefits we derive. We practically control the variety or strain of the drones of our apiary. We also procure straighter and more uniform combs. I think we need have no fears that its use in our surplus receptacles, will injure the reputation of our comb-honey. I used it several years, and that too, a bungling, illy made, article, in full sheets in all my sections, when not a person in my county knew there existed such an article, and from the sales of many hundred pounds of honey built upon it, I never heard but one word that signified the least suspicion of anything new, and very many were the praises of my "excellent comb-honey." When using it in full sheets in brood frames, I most earnestly advise wiring the frames, and I care not what kind of foundation you are using. more or less of sagging, warping or twisting is likely to injure the beauty and usefulness of your combs, if wires are not used. I find them of advantage in many other ways, and no detriment, in any. The following gives our method of

WIRING FRAMES

by hand. It cannot be pressed onto the wires as smoothly and perfectly as if done by the press, but it can be done so well th it after the bees get through manipulating it, it is in every way as perfect as if done by the machine.

When your frame material is out, and before nailed up, punch holes (centrally) through the top and bottom bars about two inches apart, and have the outside holes not further from the end bar than one-half or three-fourths of an inch. Use No. 30 tinned wire. Now sew the frame, beginning in the middle and sewing each way with each end. To fasten the ends I use a small tack, or the nails that nail the bottom-bar may be left a little out. Be careful not to draw the bottom-bar bowing by drawing the wire too tight. Diagonal wires may be put in, but I do not use them, as I find no need for them. To use them fasten one end to the tack or nail-head, and then go down through the first hole, and through the one nearest the centre of the other bar, then up through the other centre hole, and fasten this end the same as the first. Now the frame is wired.

Next make a lap-board longer each way than your frame is the longest way. Now cut from one-half inch lumber a board that is one-fourth inch smaller each way than the inside measure of your frame. Nail this board securely to the seven-eighths lap-board, and let the grains run crossways of each other. This will prevent warping. With a sponge or a rag wet the thin board or form. Have already-cut some sheets of foundation one-fourth less in size than your frame measures inside. Turn up about 3-16 of an inch on one edge, (have the wax sheet warm) and with a stiff, broad putty-knife, or chisel, mash the turned-up portion to the top-bar (which should not be rough), so that the sheet will hang centrally in the frame. We have a rest fixed for the frame, on our work bench, to hold it while we do the mashing. Next lay the frame and foundation (foundation down) on the lap-board and over the form, and while the sheet is plastic, push the wires down into the base of the cells. This can be done with an eight-penny nail; some use a wheel with points upon it. I have had success with the wire imbedder with about ten points, about one-fifth of an inch apart, the points being about one-lifth wide and one-sixty-fourth thick, so adjusted that they roll lengthwise of the wire, while each point runs crosswise of the wire. Of course they are not properly points. This puts the wire in quite rapidly and satisfactorily.

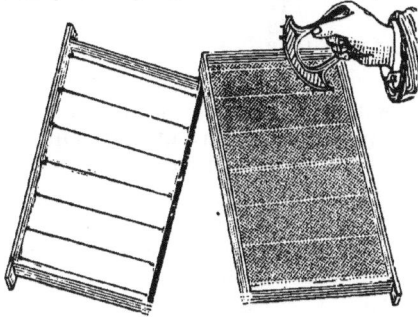

SECTIONS.

Briefly stated, my experience with sections has been, that I can get as much if not more surplus honey stored in those holding not more than one pound, than in any larger size. The reasons may be that when they are not higher than four and one-fourth inches, the bees more readily go to their tops to start work in the supers. However this may be, they are better adapted to the " tiering up " method, a method that in my opinion, has no equal, and sooner or later, will be adopted by all honey producers. This size section (4¼x4¼) sells in the markets better than any other size. It is rare indeed, that we ever hear a customer calling for larger size sections of honey. I find that I can produce just as much comb-honey in one-half pound sections as in any larger size, and that there is a demand for a portion of this size, even at a price in proportion to their extra cost of production; but those who retail or job out their crop, should only use a lesser proportion of this size, as their cost is ten to fifteen per cent. greater than the cost of one-pound sections, partly owing to the extra manipulation. I think we have a standard in the 4¼x4¼ section, but just now the question is being discussed as to the best width for these sections. During the past three years, my students and myself, have experimented considerably upon this point, and we have settled down on one and three-fourths inch, scant, or " seven to the foot," as the best width to use, whether they are used with separators or not. After we had determined a preference for the above width, with separators, we supposed that of course, one and one-half inch, or " eight to the foot," would be best where no separators were used, but actual trial on a large scale, by myself and others, demonstrated that the " seven to the foot " were the best, with or without separators.

I prefer a four-piece section, "dovetailed" or notched at all corners, made of white poplar and having openings at both top and bottom, extending their entire length. So far I have been unable to procure them, of such workmanship, as would suit those who know the importance of nice sections, short of the New England states.

29	30	31	1	2	3	4			Renewed.		
28						5					
27						6					
26						7					
25			*			8		3–4		*		1–4
24						9					
23						10		·			
22						11					
21						12					
20	19	18	17	16	15	14	13		1–2		

HEDDON'S SURPLUS HONEY REGISTER.

The above is a sample of our surplus honey register, which was suggested by seeing the queen register invented, I think, by Mr. A. I. Root, of Medina, Ohio. It embraces the essential principles of his, but I think is in a more practical shape and much more useful for surplus honey than queen registering. I agree with "My Friend," regarding the superiority of the little boards, and pencil, for the latter purpose. We make these registers of thin, white paper, to be pasted on the north side of our supers, upper back corner, or of heavy manilla paper and tack on in the same place. I rather prefer the thin paper, pasted, and they cost less, though perhaps in some cases it would be better to use the heavy article tacked to the wood. After fastening to the super, drive a cheap, soft metal No. 2 pin (such as we usually buy for five cents a paper) into the wood at the points designated by the two stars. To govern the distance to drive them, and to insure driving them straight, we make a block five inches long, one-half inch thick and seven-eighths wide and exactly square. About one inch from one end, on one side of this block with a try square we cut square across, a small groove, sufficient to receive the body of the pin. Lay your pin in this groove, placing your thumb over it to hold it firmly; place the point at the star, the edge of the block resting firmly against the super, and with a light hammer drive the head of the pin down even with the block; remove the block, bend the pin at right angles and it forms a perfect dial which will remain in place for years. We use a register on each and every super, and when we adjust such super to the hive, say May 20, we turn the head of the pin within the figures to the number "20" and the other to the letter "R" in the word "Renewed." Now you can see at a glance, rods away, that you put that super on the hive the twentieth (you can always tell the month from memory), and that it has never been looked into since. Should you now look into it on the twenty-seventh and find no work had yet been done, turn the date pin to "27" and the other to the letter "d." After this you can tell at a glance that the super had nothing in on the twenty-seventh, when it was examined which was not the day it was first given to the colony. So "R" and "d" both mean empty. Now at anytime in the future when you examine the super, turn the date pin to the day of examination and the other to a position in the circle in proportion to the accumulation of honey in the super, as you can estimate it at a glance, whether it be one-eighth, one-sixth or one-fourth, or five-eighths or seven-eighths, as the case may be. You are not confined to the positions indicated by the fractions on the register, which are merely put there for marks of division.

At a low estimate these registers save me at least, twenty-five dollars worth of labor each season. I cannot see how those who manage large numbers of hives can do without some such registering device. They are equally useful for comb or extracted honey.

SCREEN–HOUSE.

As stated by " My Friend," we much prefer the screen-house or permanent bee-tent, to those commonly advised, which are portable. All things considered, I would rather carry my "Readily Movable Hives " to my screen-house, than to carry the portable tent and place over them. I will give you a few reasons for my preference.

We rarely need either, when we have surplus upon the hives. In the few cases that we do, we prefer to set it off, quickly and securely covering it; carry the body hive, or both, to the screen-house as circumstances may demand. A screen-house will be larger and more convenient in shape and structure than a portable tent. Ours is six feet square, perfectly bee-tight, with double wire-cloth all around the upper half. The double wire cloth will not admit of the inside bees feeding those without, which practice is one of the greatest stimulants to robbing. Two of the entire sides of the house are on hinges, and when swung open every bee leaves instantly. The top is lined with cloth, with tight board roof over all. We find this an excellent place to leave our filled supers until the few adhering bees desert them. But here comes our greatest objection to the portable tent. When robbing is rife in the apiary, after removing the tent from the colony you have had open, the robbers at once pitch into it with much the same determination as when no tent has been used. They know just where to make the attack; it is not so at all when carried from the screen-house, the point of attack always remains at the place of manipulation and the hive is carried back to its own peaceful location.

Sometimes after clearing out the house, leaving nothing to rob, we open the doors slightly until the bulk of the robbers have passed in and keep them there until the bees almost cease their flying, when we let them out; well punished, and I believe somewhat repentant of their bad habits; at the same time learning which colonies are the most inclined to this vexatious habit, which gives us a chance to doctor or re-queen them. We have used both kinds of protection for three years and think we have no more use for bee-tents.

(Heddon's Feeder, Old Style.)

BEE-FEEDERS.

The compliment that " My Friend " has paid to my large bee-feeder, though it may seem extravagant to some, is one that has been given it by nearly every bee-keeper who has tested it. Since last season's improvements (which have never been on the market) it seems to me as though the implement was nearly perfection. I cannot speak of these late improvements without mentioning the names of J. L. Stevens and Benjamin Guest, two of my students, and William Stolley, my last season's superintendent, all of whom rendered material assistance in perfecting the feeder shown in the foregoing cut, "old style."

By a comparison between the above cut and the one which follows, I think the reader will recognize some valuable improvements. While we covered the old style with the hive cover, we have devised a special cover that affords conveniences much in advance of its extra cost.

By referring to the cut, you will notice that it is supplied with a central sliding piece that opens to the large central reservoir, and while opening it up with merely a touch, it closes as readily and in such a manner, that no scent of the food can escape. The act of filling this feeder does not crack the propolis placed about the joints where it is fitted to the hive or cover, by the bees, which makes it odor tight. The advantages of a central reservoir and entrances on either side, and feeding places on each side of the reservoir, must be enjoyed to be fully appreciated.

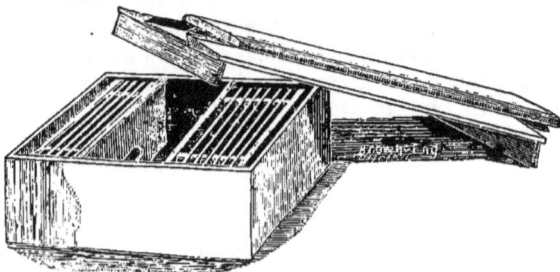

(Heddon's Feeder. New Style.)

I do not think that it is necessary to consume space giving a mechanical description, embracing measurements of all parts of the feeder. As of hives, the same may be said of this feeder. The most laborious and space consuming description, would no more than lead the average bee-keeper no construct one just enough different to leave out some important feature. A perfect sample to work by, is the only safe guide; the only one which the inventor, who takes any pride in his inventions, feels safe in giving to the general public.

I am pleased to leave this useful implement to the test and decision of my brother bee-keepers. ·

The cut above is imperfect, in so far as the feeding places on either side of the reservoir are made to appear of different capacity, and the partitions next the reservoir should come up flush with the top of the feeder.

THE PARKER FOUNDATION FASTENER.

When comb-foundation was first invented, some little trouble was experienced from the want of some quick, reliable method of attaching it to the top-bars of brood-frames and surplus section boxes.

After experimenting with molten wax, preparations of wax and rosin, different kinds of glue as well as saw cuts to pinch it fast, it was found that nothing would secure bees-wax to wood, as quickly and permanently as to press or mash it into the grains of the wood with a putty-knife or chisel. Learning this fact, we would lay our sheet of foundation into the section, passing its edge about one-eighth of an inch beyond the line we wished it to hang from, and with a putty-knife mash this one-eighth of an inch fast to the top-bar of the section; now turn the wax sheet at right angles just where it attaches to the wood, and your sheet of foundation will hang centrally in the little section frame.

We found it necessary to have our foundation sheet of a temperature of about 90 degrees Fahrenheit, and the putty knife coated with honey. By further reference to the cut you will see how the little Fastener does the work of fastening one sheet of foundation into one section, by a single motion.

The lever piece needs an occasional coating of honey, and the foundation should be tempered, as above.

You will notice that the hinges to the lever are so adjusted that after the pressure becomes great enough, said lever will begin to slide backward, the pressure all the time increasing, and this feature, which I believe originated with Mr. Parker, is what gives me a decided preference for his style of machine. One might imagine that this process would work better upon rough than smooth wood surfaces; such, however, is not the case. The smoother the wood, the better.

Bingham & Hetherington Uncapping Knife

Patented May 20, 1879.

THE HONEY KNIFE.

The Honey Knife, which is used almost exclusively for uncapping combs for extraction, is no small factor among the many necessary implements for the bee-keeper.

Very well do I remember the trials and tribulations necessarily endured while using various styles of Honey Knives, before possessing the one shown in the above cut. If we used a narrow blade we were free from the troubles accruing from dragging down the cells, caused by suction whenever our wide blades passed along their surface; but we had to suffer the great inconvenience arising from the fact that a narrow blade would not carry the cappings, but allowed them to pass over the top of the knife and stick fast in the honey just uncapped, when another motion or two would be required to remove the cappings. Wide or narrow be our blade, one serious drawback or the other must be endured.

The inventive genius of Bingham & Hetherington gave us a broad blade, with a straight bevel on the under edge of the blade (all knives prior to this were beveled on top), which gave us the narrowest bearing against the ends of the uncapped cells, together with the widest top surface for carrying away the cappings. This is not all. This lower bevel necessitates carrying the blade in a considerably arched position, which also aids in carrying the cappings, and makes the blade almost perfection itself for the purpose of neatly and quickly uncapping sunken spots that are sometimes found in the surface of combs. When I first beheld this new knife I felt very confident, and so expressed myself to Mr. Bingham, that it would not work well and satisfactorily. A half hour's practical use of it quickly convinced me to the contrary, and I was not long studying into the whys and wherefores of the perfection of its work.

This valuable acquisition to our useful implements was patented May 20th, 1879, by virtue of which it has been made of the very best material, by finished workmen, and sold at the very reasonable price of $1.00 each, by Bingham & Hetherington, of Abronia, Mich., as well as by nearly all our leading supply dealers, who could not but recognize its superiority.

Bee Veil.

FACE PROTECTORS.

The plain black bobbinet veil, as illustrated in the above cut, I believe to be—all things considered—the best and most practical, as well as cheapest, Face Protector now known to bee-keepers. It is light, and instantly adjustable to almost any hat, making it convenient to carry in the pocket when going to visit, or work other apiaries. A bee veil should never be any color but black, as all other shades are more or less difficult to see through clearly. Round meshes are also preferable to clear vision, when looking through them.

THE LAMP NURSERY.

The above cut represents the Lamp Nursery, for hatching queen cells, which is described on page 28, in chapter on Queen Rearing.

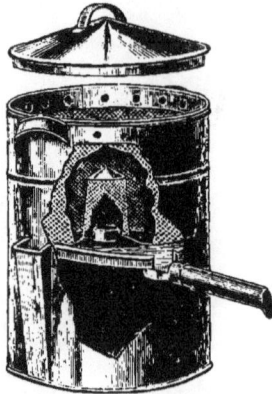

THE WAX EXTRACTOR.

We herewith illustrate this convenient utensil, described by "My Friend" on page 54. We, too, have found them rather small and slow of operation where hundreds of pounds of wax were to be rendered at one time; but as very few modern bee-keepers will have any such amount of wax making to do in the future, I can recommend these Extractors because of their handiness and perfect cleanliness in storing up and melting smaller quantities of comb, which slowly but surely accumulates in all apiaries.

WHITMAN FOUNTAIN PUMP.

Above is shown the Whitman Fountain Pump, spoken of by "My Friend" on page 55. These pumps are made of best material, and the workmanship is excellent. They are not only very useful to the bee-keeper, in the ways mentioned on page 55, but in very many other particulars outside of the demands of the apiary. They are excellent with which to wash windows, outside; very useful in cleaning buggies; they do quite good work in sprinkling lawns, and gardens; they have saved many buildings, by extinguishing fires in their incipiency. The bee-keeper cannot afford to do without at least one, in his apiary.

SHIPPING CRATES.

The above cut is a perfect representation of our preferred Shipping Crate, except that the engraver has made the bottom, which is nailed on the outside, look as though it was larger than the Crate, which it is not, but of its exact outside dimensions, the same as the cover.

The first Crate I ever saw, was glassed on its sides, rather than ends, and the grooves were made in the ends of the solid end pieces, which received a glass as long as the Crate the longest way, and as wide as the crate was high. This style of glassing crates was quite expensive, and I found unnecessarily so. I changed the method of glassing at once, cutting my grooves in the edges of the cleats, thus using glasses not over one-half the width. I found by experience in shipping several tons of comb honey in these Crates that there was no need for any more glass than just enough to show the kind and quality of the contents of the crate. That secured safety in handling, and satisfaction to the observer. Next, I changed the cleats and glass to the ends, instead of side of the Crates, for the following reasons:

1st. The Crate would be stronger, and cheaper.

2nd. The cleats would serve as handles, at the same time allowing us to handle the Crate, side to us, with combs ranging to and from us.

3rd. When made in this manner, the Crate is just as long as our storing cases are wide (which is a plump foot), and so whatever size section we use, of which the width of any given number measure one foot, thus perfectly fitting our storing cases, the same will equally fit our Shipping Crates.

Our one-half pound sections are of such dimensions from front to rear, that six of them measure just the same as four of the 4¼ sections, viz.: Seventeen inches. All are just 4¼ inches high. You will see that the Crate whose width is adapted to two of the 4¼ sections is equally well adapted to three of the half pound sections. Thus we have a small, solid shipping crate that receives 12, 4¼x4¼x2 sections, which are six to the foot; 14 of the same, seven to the foot; 16 of the same, eight to the foot; 21 of the half pounds, seven to the foot; 24 of the same, eight to the foot, and all of these five sizes perfectly fitting the Crate.

We make our Shipping Crates of white basswood, but pine or poplar will answer very well for the purpose. I advise small Shipping Crates, as safest in which to transport comb honey, and readiest of sale when placed upon the market.

The question of a combined Storing Case and Shipping Crate, is one that has been discussed much, and experimented with a little. It is one of the subjects that I can satisfactorily decide upon, for myself, without the trouble and expense of a trial. I feel confident that honey thus produced and negligently sent to market, would never do for my trade.

Among the many objections to storing and selling comb honey in the same case, or crate (whichever it may be called), I will enumerate a few:

1st. A good Storing Case—one up to the modern standard—is not only inferior to the Shipping Crate above illustrated, in nearly every respect, but is too costly to be given away with honey sales; and any system of selling, that confines itself to charging for or recovering the Crates, will not stand commercial test.

2nd. Comb honey is sought largely for its fine appearance, as is proven by its commanding double the price of equally choice extracted honey, after twenty years of acquaintance with consumers. This fact enjoins us to neglect nothing that will improve the appearance of our surplus combs.

To ship sections to market—that is, any market that pays good prices—just as they are left by the bees, would be to lose many times more than it costs to remove them from cases to crates, cleaning them of all propolis, when crating.

The producer should grade his combs, know just what each Crate contains, and represent it just as it is. Regarding this matter, I feel confident that "the longest way around is the nearest way across."

CHAPTER XXII.

Patents.—Are they Necessary?

The above is a question that I have frequently asked, both in private conversation and through the Bee Journal. I believe there is a misconception upon the part of many, regarding the spirit of our Patent Laws. You will often hear men, who claim and mean to be honest, say to an inventor regarding his invention, " Is this patented?" and upon learning that it is not, continue by saying, " Then I will manufacture some of them."

The questioner evidently entertains the idea that an inventor has an exclusive right to a patented article only after, and because, he has paid the government $35.00. I think this is a great mistake. Every civilized nation grants to an inventor an exclusive right to his invention for a term of years, because it recognizes that such an exclusive right belongs to him, which should be paid, because justice demands it, and to stimulate invention for the benefit of its people. It recognizes that in the mental, as well as the physical world, one has a right to at least part of the results of his own labor. The thirty-five dollars is merely the recording fee demanded, to support the office.

The government makes no patent laws to aid extortion from her people, but to protect inventors in their natural rights. Had the first speaker in the above dialogue rightly understood this matter, would he not have said, "Will you object to my making and using your invention?" "Can I borrow the results of your labor!" I once entertained the idea that possibly these principles could be so thoroughly inculcated into the minds of the members of our fraternity, that they would all respect each inventor of implements in our line, patent or no patent. But experience has taught me that in our business, as in others, a few there are, who will do right only when forced to. For this class, the Patent Laws, like all other laws, are made.

The patent system is the pride of inventors and honest people in general, but the dread of him who wishes to purloin the labors of another without giving an equivalent.

On page 620 of Gleanings in Bee Culture, its editor, Mr. Root, pens the following moral gem, which will make his name remembered by all men of intelligence and integrity. He says:

"I am very glad indeed to note the disposition among bee-keepers of forbearing to copy the works of each other, patent or no patent. The supply dealer who would unhesitatingly copy something well known to be the property of another, without getting the privilege of doing so, by purchase or otherwise, would very likely lose more than he made, so strong is the disposition of our people to give honor to whom honor is due."

In the same periodical on page 179—1885—our state entomologist, Prof. A. J. Cook, says of the above: "I wish to commend what you say about inventions. We should respect them, whether patented or not."

I now believe patents are necessary to the fulfillment of justice, and best interests of our people.

I have had some recent personal experience, regarding the boldness with which some of our people will appropriate the work of another, even when requested not to do so. In two instances that have come to my notice, hive manufacturers have wronged me knowingly. To one, I gave complete samples, free of charge, with the understanding that he was to sell at prices quoted in my circular, furnishing equally good workmanship, etc. These promises were not carried out. He made a reduction in the price, and a still greater one in quality.

After I had patiently and persistently labored to establish a reputation for accurate, honest work, another advertised "Heddon's Hives," and sent out material in the flat, so inaccurate in dimensions as to be practically valueless to the purchaser. Who suffered by this transaction?

I felt as though my inventions, although not patented, should be respected; that I should be consulted regarding their character and introduction.

The control of the manufacture of an article, should not, and does not, in the nature of things, tend to increase its price. This control enables the manufacturer, by virtue of his greater volume of business, to not only employ the very best workmanship and material, but to turn out the goods at minimum cost. This secures to him a fair compensation, at the same time adding nothing to the outlay of the consumer.

Another point is that no man has as much pride in the excellence of the construction of an article, as does the inventor—he who has a pride and interest in its introduction. It is not he, but the imitator who is ignorant and careless of the proper bearing, adjustment and construction of the new article. His only aim is profit; to-day's profit, regardless of the profits of the future.

It is a duty, and I assure you a pleasure for me to say that I have every reason to believe that a vast majority of our bee-keepers, need no patent laws to force them to justice. I am mindful of the many substantial encouragements I have received, as an inventor.

Mr. A. I. Root requested the privilege of illustrating and describing my old hive, honey board, etc., in his paper, and manufacturing the same to supply the demand of his customers. To him, as to every person who in like manner recognized justice in the matter, all he asked was granted, without money and without price. Mr. Root, however, sent me $100 as a token of appreciation.

Messrs. McKallep, Margrave & Co., proprietors of the Hiawatha, Kansas, bee-hive manufactory, in like manner sent me $10, wishing to manufacture my inventions, upon which they, too, knew I had procured no legal exclusive right.

Do not such men as these deserve our highest respect, and will they not receive it?

It has been said that our inventions are merely mental evolutionary growths. I grant it. The patent laws will grant to each inventor just that part of that growth which belongs to him—and no more. Suppose Mr. B. discovers a principle, but fails to make a practical application of the same. Mr. A. does likewise. C. looks at both, and discovers a third, which makes the first two of value to humanity. He gets the right. He is the real benefactor of mankind.

Again it is said that if Mr. C. did not discover and monopolize the discovery, it would be left in the great secret vault of Nature, where it would soon be discovered by another. I grant that. I used to think that this was one valid argument against the patent system (not patentees); but let us look at it further: The objection raised is, that when Father Langstroth took from this great "vault" his movable frame, he robbed it of one great truth, and thus left us one less chance to discover; and had he not done so, we would, ere this, have found it. I grant and believe the last part of that sentence, but not the first. Truths are infinite in number. No matter what A, B or C takes from the vault, there is an infinity left, and I found that a thought of this depletion arose from a stronger desire to take what some one else had groped about after in the darkness, and finally laid outside the vault door, than to go in likewise and meritoriously bring something else to light. When Father L. held his patent ("monopoly"), we are told there was much effort made to rob him of the results of his labor. One hive vender, who was infringing his patent, after doing so with a set determination; going into lawsuits with him, trying to prove priority with this same old story, "used by Mr. M. years ago," and failing, proposed a relief fund, which he headed with $100. Father L. rose in his dignity and genius, and said: "Sir, I will not accept one cent from you. I only ask what belongs to me."

All of this is about the patent system, and not patentees. A reason why Brown has a moral as well as legal right to patent his inventions, is because living under the patent system, he always has paid and likely always will pay a tribute to the inventions of others.

My main objection to the patent system has been the money lost by the purchase of worthless inventions. Yet we should not forget the old verse which says:

> "Some people, if they had their pleasure,
> Because silly bargains are made;
> Would deem it a rational measure,
> To lay an embargo on trade."

Patent or no patent, we should always avoid buying worthless goods, worthless either in principal or construction.

Some have come to believe that whoever asks money for a Patent Right, is an extortionist. I think we have shown that the inventor has a right to his inventions, the results of his labor. If he has, he certainly has the right to sell them in such manner, and at such price as he shall dictate, we reserving the right to purchase or not, as we think best.

The same laws that govern all other lines of traffic are all that are needed to govern this.

Father Langstroth's patent, supplied him with means to introduce his valuable inventions to the public.

Two years before its expiration, his agent came to me and found me with hives without movable frames. For the purpose of obtaining $10 for an individual right, and I presume of enjoying the pleasure of doing good to his fellow men, this agent carefully and minutely explained to me the superiority of his hive and system of management. I was able to discover it at once, and glad to exchange the $10 for what within those two years, proved to be worth hundreds of dollars to me.

CHAPTER XXIII.

Hives.

No adequate consideration of the progress of invention as applied to Bee-Hives, in connection with modern apiculture, can for one moment ignore the genius of Rev. L. L. Langstroth, for it was his invention that first made bee-culture a possible, paying business. Some idea of how intimately associated with success in our chosen pursuit, is this question of Hives, may be gained when we reflect upon the fact, that thousands of patents have been issued upon "improved" Hives, and yet our most successful apiarists are still seeking for a Hive better adapted to maximum production at minimum cost. Necessity is said to be "the mother of invention." Certain it is, that the low prices of our products has compelled the specialist to seek by every possible means, to lessen the cost of its production. An important factor in this problem is the amount of labor required for the attainment of definite results. For many years past I have experimented largely with a view of lessening the labor of necessary manipulation in the apiary; of devising some method whereby in one hour, I might accomplish what had hitherto required two. While conducting these experiments, I ascertained that nearly all the necessary manipulation of bees, might be better and far more speedily accomplished by handling Hives more and frames less; that many "short cuts" to the desired end, might be easily made, that were wholly impossible with the L. frame. I also learned the great importance of a proper adjustment of combs and the working force, in the attainment of best results; of the necessity of Hives that would admit of easy, rapid manipulation, capable of being expanded or contracted at will, yet avoiding all extra fixtures and complication. I am happy to say that my new Hive embodies all these, and more desirable features. It has been thoroughly tested by different persons, under varying conditions, who agree with me in the claim, that the results attending its use have hitherto been unattainable.

On going into detail with this very important subject, I will first describe the L. Hive, as modified and used by myself; a modification which has become quite popular with many of our most successful Honey producers. In recounting my efforts to arrange and manipulate this Hive in such manner as to obtain the very best results with the least labor, you will see how I was led to the invention and adoption of the New Hive.

The above cut represents my modification of the Langstroth Hive. For several years, I used the old standard L. Hive, containing 10 frames, and portico. Since changing to 8 frames, and doing away with the portico, supplying it with the cleat and Bottom-stand, F, it has given me much better satisfaction, for the production of both comb and extracted honey.

Above the top of the brood chamber is shown my Honey Board G.

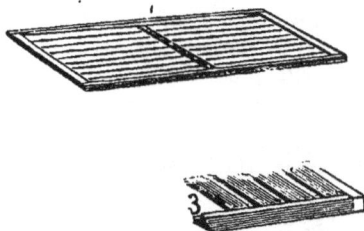

I will pause to describe this Honey Board, which I deem a necessity to the easy manipulation of the Hive, and ever neat, clean condition of the surplus sections.

It is constructed of slats, so arranged that the upper surface of the Board contains a Bee space. There is a narrow rim all around the outer edge, which receives the lower side of all surplus receptacles, leaving a Bee space between their lower surface, and the general top surface of the Honey Board. This general surface is composed of slats, so arranged as to leave just eight ⅜ inch slots for Bee passage ways, running lengthwise of the hive and frames, one slot exactly over the center of each top bar below, and extending its entire length. I consider this Honey Board as my most valuable invention connected with the above Hive. Reports from many of our oldest and most practical Honey producers, who have thoroughly tested it, have corroborated this opinion, formed by ten years of experience, giving it the most rigid tests. It is in no way a detriment, either to the bees or bee-master. We have found queen excluding Honey Boards a practical success, and this Honey Board can be made

queen excluding by simply widening the slats, to such width as to contract
the bee-passages between them to too small a space to admit of the passage of the queen. The perforated zinc queen excluding metal can be
used in place of the slats, still retaining the bee space in the Honey Board,
and in some respects this metal is superior.

That successful producer, and eminent writer, Mr. W. Z. Hutchinson,
was the first to make my Honey Board queen excluding, by arranging its slats so as to leave only passage-ways too small to admit the queen.

I was nearly three years satisfying myself that these narrow passage-
ways were in no way detrimental to the rapid storing of surplus honey,
and during all this time spent in experimenting with about sixty queen
excluding Honey Boards, I have been continually discovering more and
more advantages to be derived from their use. It now seems certain that
they are to unfold still more aids to our pursuit, yet unthought of. I am
quite positive that they are going to aid us greatly in queen rearing, as I
find that the Bees will tolerate two queens, or cells and queens, in the
same hive, at all times in the season, if divided by these queen excluding
Honey Boards. I think they may yet settle the drone and swarming
question.

The under side of our Honey Board has an even surface, and when
placed on the hive, rests bee space above the tops of the movable frames,
because they rest ⅜ of an inch below the top edge of the hive. This is one
of Father Langstroth's inventions, and in my estimation best of them all,
and one always to be used by the mass of our Honey producers. To better describe its value, I will quote from the specifications of his patent
papers, long since expired. Regarding this invaluable

BEE SPACE,

or shallow air chamber above the frames, he says:

"The apertures or bee passages in the Honey Board may be made
without being liable to be closed by the bees, as they so frequently are in
hives which have not this shallow air space. It will be seen that the bees
can pass into this shallow chamber from between all the ranges of comb,
and from the front and rear walls of the hive, and sides of the frames,
without even passing through the combs at all, and that they can pass
from the shallow chamber into any of the honey receptacles, without, as
in other hives, losing much time in the height of the honey harvest by
crowding through populous combs or contracted passages.

This shallow chamber, while it greatly facilitates the storage of honey in large receptacles, is specially adapted to securing it in small ones,
which usually meet with the readiest sale.

1st. The building of comb requires the bees to maintain a high temperature, and they work to the best advantage when they can economize
their animal heat; but this they cannot do in small receptacles, which
communicate with the hive through such apertures as are usually made
in its top, such apertures not admitting freely the heat and odor from
the main colony, and the bees in a small receptacle being too few to keep
up the requisite temperature. The shallow chamber, however, like the
part of a room nearest the ceiling, is in the storing season always full of
the warmest air of the hive—thus aiding to keep the smallest receptacles
full of the same.

If the large openings or bee passages are made in hives having no
shallow chamber, for the purpose of giving a freer admission into small
receptacles, of the heat and odor of the hive, the bees often connect the
combs of the surplus receptacles with those of the main hive, making it
difficult to remove the surplus honey in a proper condition, and the queen

being thus able to travel over the combs into the receptacles is much more liable to enter them for breeding, than she is where the interposition of the shallow air space would require her to leave the combs.

2.1. Bees always desire to work in large numbers, so that they can easily intercommunicate with each other, and the common arrangement for inducing them to work in small receptacles, is opposed to this instinct. whereas the shallow chamber affords a place of repose for multitudes of bees engaged in secreting the wax to be used in the surplus receptacles. and as a succession of bees are thus constantly ascending and descending, they work in small receptacles with scarcely more isolation, and with almost as much rapidity, as though they were merely filling the upper part of their main hive.

This shallow chamber answers other highly important purposes: (a) It prevents the bees from cementing the cover or honey board to the tops of the frames or bars, thus enabling it to be more easily removed when access is wanted to the combs. (b) It enables the cover to be put over the frames or bars with much less danger of crushing bees than if it rested on their tops. (c) It permits the bees, when the cover is on, to pass from comb to comb above the tops of the frames or bars. (d) It aids to keep a feeder in cool weather filled with the warmest air of the hive. (e) It gives an air space between the combs and the cover, thus more effectually guarding the bees against extremes of heat and cold. (f) It enables us to give the bees better protection against dampness in their hives, as by leaving the apertures in the cover open, in cold weather, there is a much freer escape of moisture than when the cover rests flat upon the frames or bars."

The above, written by Father Langstroth, more than thirty years ago, clearly sets forth most of the great advantages of this air space in our hives, which, after the progress made by the fraternity during this whole period, is still considered indispensible by our most successful apiarists, almost without exception.

My Honey Board, as above described, containing a bee space within itself, is, so far as I know, the only one which is so constructed as to be perfectly adapted to brood chambers and surplus receptacles so arranged that they can be used together without the Honey Board, preserving proper bee spaces, etc.

I can assure my readers that several extensive critical tests have proven beyond all doubt that the use of such a Honey Board in no way tends to discourage the bees from entering the surplus receptacles.

During three different seasons, when our apiaries numbered hundreds of colonies, unexpected outside demands for these Honey Boards compelled us to do without them upon about one-half of our hives, giving us a perfect test of their usefulness and postive proof that they cause no detrimental effects, while the break-joint principle, i. e., the arrangement of the slats of the Honey Board, so that their centers come directly over the passages between the brood frames, almost totally does away with the mussy attachments of brace combs to the surplus receptacles above, and leaves a perfect communication or passage for the heat and odor of the hive, as well as the working bees.

Next above the Honey Board is shown my

SURPLUS CASE,

D, which contains 28 sections, 4¼x4¼x1¾ scant, or "7 to the foot." I believe this to be the best possible style of surplus receptacle, to be used without separators. It seems to me to be very nearly perfect. I am satisfied that I cannot make an improvement upon it. I have never seen one suggested, that I thought was not a detriment. However, I think them illy adapted to the use of separators. They are constructed the same exterior size of the top of the hive, of thin material, with divisions between the tiers of sections which are as wide as the height of the sections, (4¼ inches) while the sides and ends of the cases are ⅞ inch, or bee space higher than the divisions and sections. Tin strips at the bottom, where all pieces are even, are tacked on in such manner as to hold the sections from sliding out of true position:

We use no glass, or outer covering to these cases, having proven by experiment, that all such are worse than useless.

From two, to four of these cases (usually about three) are used on our hives at one time. They are worked upon what is known as the

TIERING-UP SYSTEM,

which is as follows: When the surplus harvest seems to be opening (which can be determined by the appearance of small pieces of new brace combs, built between the tops of the frames and cover of the hive) we place the Honey Board on the hive (bee space side up) and now one case on the Honey Board, turning the dial pins as directed on page 64. In a few days we may find this case of sections nearly two-thirds full of honey, especially if they were well filled with comb foundation. We now proceed to lift it off, which is a very easy task, as the narrow edges of the case are all that touch the Honey Board, and the bee space, above the slats, arranged on the break-joint principle, have prevented the attachment of brace combs or propolis between the sections and anything below them. We now place another case on the Honey Board (adjusting the register), and place the partly filled case upon the empty one, also adjusting its register showing the date, and estimated amount of surplus it contains.

If the honey flow is good, in a few days another case may be needed to give the bees room to do their best, even before all the combs of the first, or upper case, are entirely capped. Now we adjust a third case, as before, always putting the empty cases on the Honey Board. It is quite likely that before more room will be needed by the bees, the upper case first adjusted will be completed, when it can be removed and another empty one placed under the other two, as before, and so on. This is the Tiering-up System, and in my judgment the one destined to become universally adopted. As the surplus combs are about to be capped, this system places them in such a position to the brood-chamber, as to facilitate speedy finishing, and bright, clean work, as bees often soil white combs by constantly traveling over them. especially when moving directly to them, from the darker combs of the brood-chamber. Again, opening a gap or empty space between the brood-chamber of the hive, and what surplus the bees have already made, seems to stimulate them to fill it (thus connecting the apartments, with their work), just as soon as possible.

Having thus outlined this Tiering system, I will describe our method of ridding the filled cases of the bees that adhered to them when removed from the hives. When removing them from the hives, by a judicious use of smoke at the top, we drive more than four-fifths of the bees down into the lower cases, and then we take the case by its handles and by a quick, trembling motion, we shake nearly all of the remaining bees down in front of the hive. We now carry the case, with its 50 to 100 remaining bees, to the screen house, where we stand it on end, freely admitting the light into the spaces between the combs from either side, when within a half hour the last bee will have gone to the wire screen.

The sides of this hive are ⅞, the ends ⅝, bottom and cover ⅜ inch, which thicknesses we prefer to thicker material, for other reasons besides that it aids in making it a

READILY MOVABLE HIVE.

I believe the honey production of the future will demand light, "Readily Movable Hives." When one comes to manage large apiaries, pushing business upon that scale which necessitates dispatch, he will find this Readily Movable feature of more value than all the advantages derived from such features as necessitate making hives cumbersome.

Our methods of preventing after-swarms, or increase from the same, making increase artificially, as well as many other manipulations, appreciate such hives.

I believe that cellar, or other repository wintering, will be the general practice of the future. Here again the same demand is repeated.

I feel that I cannot urge too strongly against the use of hives that embrace any telescoping principle, i. e., so constructed as to have one story over-lap another, so that one cannot be removed from the other by a lateral movement, but must be raised up, and let down, when removing or readjusting. There should never be a dead air space or double covering over the surplus room. Sections should never rest upon each other or on the brood frames. The sections should always run paralel with the brood frames.

More recent experiments have proven that hives with smaller brood-chambers are better adapted to the most economical production of comb honey. Not only this, but at certain periods during the surplus season, it is highly advisable, in the production of comb honey, to still more contract the breeding department to a minimum capacity.

Among other successful comb honey producers, whose large experience has taught them to use small brood-chambers, I may mention the names of T. F. Bingham and G. M. Doolittle. On page 373 of American Bee Journal for 1884, may be found an article from the pen of Mr. Doolittle, plainly setting forth many reasons for using small brood-chambers, and at certain periods contracting them still smaller, when producing comb honey. While the objects he seeks and accomplishes are nearly identical with those sought and accomplished by the contraction method, as practiced by myself, the fixtures and consequent manipulations adopted by him seem to me much more complicated and impractical than those we have used.

Perhaps I cannot better describe the system, as we have practiced it with our modification of the Langstroth hive, than to copy an article of mine published in the American Bee Journal for 1885, page 437.

The illustration shown in this article represents my Hive as shorter from front to rear than from side to side. This is not the case, however, as its exterior dimensions are 13 inches in width and 19¾ inches in length. (See first cut in this chapter.)

"During the past three years I have been carefully testing a hive-contracting system, and I have found it of great value, as regards both summer and winter success. It has become a permanent system in my apiaries when running for comb honey, and now, after testing it for three seasons, I feel prepared to speak of what I know.

I hive all swarms, whether first or second swarms, upon five Langstroth frames of foundation, filling up the rest of the space in an 8-frame hive, with 2 contractors or "dummies," A, A, as shown in the illustration. I find that the queen uses these five combs to that extent that I get as much brood in them as in any 7 combs where the whole 8 are used. The 5 combs become nearly 5 solid sheets of brood, and where they are reversible, quite all brood. Certain it is that this contraction in no way tends to increase the amount of honey stored, but to a great extent tends to increase the amount stored as surplus, and decrease the quantity stored in the brood-chamber.

This contraction also keeps much bee-bread out of the hive, leaving it in the field, which is by far the best and most economical reservoir for it, in this locality. With this treatment, a prime swarm commences work in the cases at once; I usually place one case on the hive when hiving a swarm. A second swarm usually commences in the surplus cases in 2 or 3 days after being hived.

In autumn, when the honey harvest is over, the little brood-chamber contains but little honey and pollen (almost none at all if the bees are German). I now have much honey in the supers that without contraction would have been in the hive, and I am now ready to feed the colony sugar syrup for winter. When fed, the bees are in a condition where all their stores are accessible, and to winter with almost absolute certainty, if they are kept warm enough. Whether the brood-chambers are almost honeyless, or partially stored, depends upon the nature and duration of the honey-flow, and the blood of the bees. Most bee-keepers are aware of the fact that Italians are more prone to load the brood-chamber, regardless of the surplus department, both early and late in the season, than are the German bees.

While the system is so nearly perfected that with any bees I bring nearly all of the colonies out at the close of the season, so as to take one-half or more of their winter and spring stores through the feeder, I have it complete as far as Germans and most hybrid colonies are concerned. I am now at work with assurance of perfecting the system, so as to bring out all brood-chambers, with any bees, in a perfect starvation condition; our honey all gone into the market, and our colonies all ready to receive the winter food prepared by the bee-master, as their whole winter and spring stores. I believe that sugar syrup is better than honey as spring stores, till the weather is quite warm, and till the bees can fly daily.

I keep the bees on these 5 combs, after placing them on the summer stands, until the spreading of the queen and the advance of the sun north of the equator calls for more room, when I remove the contractors, replacing 3 combs which are put in the positions occupied by the contractors, or among the combs of brood, spreading them, according to the weather and force of the colony. When this colony swarms, I hive its swarm on 5 combs, as above described, and then on the twentieth day after swarming, I go to the old hive and find, as a rule, a young, fertile queen, eggs in the centre combs, and three or more combs with considerable honey and no brood, which I remove, replacing them with the contractors. This old colony is soon in the supers, having a 5-comb brood-chamber filled solid with brood.

I have had colonies, after casting 3 swarms, at work in the supers within 5 days after contracting. I think that the advantages of this contracting system will be seen; or it may be called an enlarging system; that is, enlarging the brood-chamber for about 6 weeks during the time that the queen is not only the most prolific, but when such prolificness gives us bees to become field-workers, just when we most need them. I think that it will also be seen, too, with what advantage reversible frames

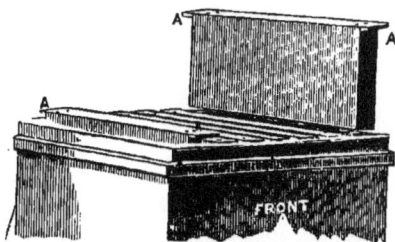

[A A shows the two Contractors—one nearly in position, and the other just ready to go down into the hive.]

may be added to this system. I make the contractors by making a wide frame just the same width all around, and just the size of the standard Langstroth brood-frame. It is no division-board, as it has all the same bee spaces as has the brood-frames, and thus manipulates very easily. When the frame is made, I nail a ½ inch board upon each side, and in the middle I place a little cubic block, a little smaller than the width of the frame; by nailing each side to this block, they will be just a little concave.

'Through all the summer days,' the contractors are kept at the same distance from the sides of the hive and adjacent combs, as the combs are kept from each other; but in winter I move them back close to the sides of the hive, thus aiding as non-conductors, and giving a little more wintering room; these two points I consider non-essentials, however.

Some of the contractors I fill with chaff, some with sawdust, and I also have 300 made of solid wood, but these are only ⅞ of an inch thick, and each pair replaces but 2 combs, leaving 6 instead of 5. When 6 are used the spaces of the honey-board exactly break joints with the spaces below, as with 8 combs; but with 5 combs I move the honey-board sidewise as much as it will go and still rest solid on the hive, and then I leave the break-joint feature of the honey-board perfect as before. It was by the use of this 5-comb system that I first got my best test of the great value of the break-joint feature of the honey-board. I never knew how much more, queens and comb would get up through where they ought not to, till after I placed a lot of honey-boards on some contracted hives, and in such a manner that the slots corresponded vertically instead of breaking joints with each other.

My first thought was to have these contractors, broad-frames filled with sections, but experience taught me, first, that we did not need any more surplus room with a Langstroth hive and complete "Tiering-up" system; second, it adds complication to have storing in sections going on in the brood-chamber; and third, the honey stored there is not fit for market, at least none that I have ever seen comes up to my standard. If it was only started there, and finished in a better place, it might do, but as such a system complicates labor still more, why should we use the place, when we have all the room we want without it, and in a far better and handier position? I have not been troubled with the queen entering the sections, when I used the honey-boards in proper position, though most of them are not queen-excluding, the slots being ⅝ of an inch, or double bee-space.

I notice that others have been cotemporary with me in working out the advantages of contracting, but so far as I have read, I have not as yet seen it systematized as a summer and winter management. I have here endeavored to so place it before my fellow bee-keepers, and I do it with the full conviction that we can and will yet still further lessen the detail labor of manipulation, and keep all the advantages of this valuable system."

The advantages to be gained from this system of contraction are very numerous, many of which were set forth by Mr. G. M. Doolittle about one year ago in the American Bee Journal. For some reason it did not at that time meet with much opposition. Whether because not clearly understood, or otherwise. I am unable to say, but since the appearance of my article as copied above, considerable opposition has been elicited. I believe that bee-keepers at large, accord with it, in the main.

In Gleanings in Bee Culture for 1885, page 94, Mr. Doolittle, in favor of the contracting system, remarks as follows, in answer to a bee-keeper, who, when running for comb honey, proposed to hive his swarms on a full hive of combs, and then extract honey from them:

"By so doing the bees found room to occupy all their forces; while if only one-half or one-third as many had been given, the bees not being able to cluster and work on these combs, would have immediately gone into the sections, and gone to work on them. Having thus at once started in the sections, the little honey stored in the few combs below will be carried to the sections as fast as the queen needs room for egg-laying, and the result with me is, that at the end of 15 days from the time of hiving, the sections are well filled with honey, and the combs below a solid mass of brood, except a little pollen and honey in the extreme upper corners of the frames. The object should be in all cases, whether you use combs, frames of foundation, or empty frames, to get the bees at work in the sections immediately upon being hived. I use six Gallup frames of comb (equal to 5 L. frames) for the very largest swarms, while others have but 4 or 5, according to the size of the swarm to be hived, and in this way I always secure good results. The greatest secret of getting comb honey is to get the sections just as near to the brood as possible; and any plan which allows of one or more inches of sealed honey between the brood and sections is certainly defective."

In the same periodical, page 513, Mr. W. Z. Hutchinson says:

"It does seem as though bees that have but little brood, and plenty of combs to fill, store twice as much honey as bees with a hive full of brood to care for."

It must be borne in mind that this system never contemplates contracting the brood-chamber to a minimum, at such time of year as when eggs are laid by the queen will grow into bees to become gatherers during any important honey harvest occurring the same season.

Many bee-keepers seem to think that it is a great mistake, resulting in financial loss, if we do not supply hive, combs, and nurse bees at any and all times of year, sufficient to mature all the eggs a prolific queen could deposit. To me this looks like the philosophy entertained by the Indian, who, having picked up a flint, concluded economy demanded that he have a gun made to it. We must remember that nearly all our capital is invested outside of the queen, and while it makes no material difference whether this capital is equal to the prolificness of the queen or not, it is very important that her prolificness should at all times during the breeding season be fully equal to this capital. Let me quote from one of my articles written several years ago:

"What is the object in a very prolific queen? The answer always comes, 'to produce the greatest number of workers.' Let us look into the matter:

If one is buying queens, they cost from one to three dollars each. What is the purpose of these purchases? Most assuredly to change the quality and not the quantity of the workers. When the apiary is satisfactorily stocked with the preferred blood, then one allows his bees to rear their own queens, and they cost not to exceed 25c. each if the bee-keeper is by selection improving his stock, and if not, not to exceed 2c. each. Now, "to get honey we want to get bees," and to get bees we must invest capital in queens, combs, hives, yard, and necessary fixtures. Allowing that the queen costs the one who produces her for his own use, 25c., and all the other fixtures $2.50 per colony, we see at once that it makes but little difference whether we have extra prolific queens or not. I do not want it understood that I approve of any queen that is abnormally unprolific, for such is not the case. I behead all such as soon as I find them. But right here I want to say that since I quit the encouragement of abnormally prolific queens, I hardly ever find one of the former class. I believe that there is a law in nature that covers the fecundity of queens, that the more the quantity (above the normal amount) the poorer the quality.

Some advise us to "have extra prolific queens; put each one in a hive containing 30 combs, then shift the combs every few days, and make her keep them full of brood." I tried it—to my satisfaction. I found that this method demanded an extra amount of labor—a labor that would pay the interest at 20 per cent, on every dollar of the capital invested. So I just cut up these large, long hives, making five out of each one, and divided those 30 combs among these hives, and reared four more queens. Now each queen kept her six combs full of brood without any "horse-whipping" whatever, and my colonies became automatic as far as breeding was concerned."

"Keep your colonies strong," has been laid down as a golden rule. If that means, keep your bees numerous in proportion to their hives and combs, I most freely accord with that rule; but on the other hand, if we are to understand that most profit will be realized from the capital and labor, when invested in colonies containing greater numbers of bees, regardless of how acquired, I must dissent from accepting the rule.

It matters little how many workers you can produce from one queen, if you must furnish brood-chamber room and many combs to be filled, each with an unknown quantity of brood, honey and bee-bread.

It is with bees as with their product, the greatest number of bees from the least capital and labor, is our object.

Make your brood-chambers automatic by constructing them of such size and shape that a normally prolific queen will occupy them almost exclusively with her brood, without any tedious manipulation on your part. In this way you will secure the greatest amount of surplus honey for the capital and labor bestowed, and can if you wish, without special effort, bring your colonies out at the close of honey gathering, with very little stores in their brood combs, when you can feed them sugar syrup for safe wintering, or you can easily manipulate them so as to have your contracted brood-chamber fully stocked with natural stores, as will be explained farther on. I will now endeavor to illustrate and describe my

REVERSIBLE FRAMES.

While the reversing of brood combs will produce no ill effects whatever, numerous are the advantages arising from such reversal; some of which aid us materially in accomplishing the desired results which are partially accomplished in the contracting system, above described.

When using frames even no deeper than the standard Langstroth, you know how the bees (especially Italians) will persist in crowding the queen by storing honey that ought to go into the surplus department, along the upper edge of the brood combs, just under the top bar, and farther down in the upper corners. till by actual measurement we find that nearly one-fourth of each frame, and sometimes more, is occupied with honey.

Now if we reverse the frame containing a comb so filled, we place the honey in an unusual position; in a place usually occupied with brood, and when this is done in the breeding season, when the bees are not inclined to decrease their quantity of brood, this honey will be immediately removed to the surplus department, and soon the frame will be one solid sheet of brood, which is a glad sight to the bee-keeper whose experience has taught him the value of a compact brood nest, free from honey.

It is also true that reversing the combs late in the season, just at the time when brood rearing is giving way to filling the cells with winter stores from the last honey yielding flowers, will equally tend toward the complete filling of the combs with honey.

But there is another decided advantage to be enjoyed by one, if never but one, reversal. After the comb is completed, and is so attached to the frame at the top and part way down the end-bars as to be satisfactory to the bees, it will be found much more satisfying to the bee-master to have such comb as perfectly attached to the entire end pieces and bottom-bar. Such a straight, all-worker comb on wires, thus solidly built, is "a thing of beauty and a joy forever" to the apiarist who has had experience with hordes of useless drones (some of inferior blood, thus much worse than useless), combs breaking down; queens hiding between the bottom of the comb and bottom-bar, bees sticking there when trying to brush and shake them from the combs, etc.

Since the subject of reversing brood-combs has been agitating the minds of bee-keepers, numerous are the styles of frames made and proposed for that purpose. It is with these frames as with hives, honey-extractors and other implements, utterly impossible to devise any one style of reversible frame that will possess all the advantages of all other styles.

About one and one-half years ago I devised the style of reversible brood-frame, as shown by the illustrations. I made 8,000 of them entirely for my own use, and succeeded in getting about one-half of them into use the first season. I have tested them two seasons, and like them well

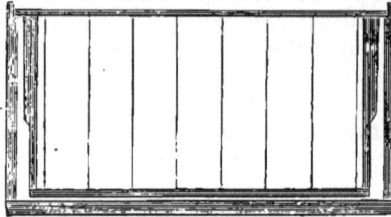

Fig. 1.

(The above cut is imperfect, as it does not show the inner top bar of the inner frame. Fig. 2 will illustrate the true construction of the frame.)

At a glance, almost any one can estimate the extra cost of constructing such a frame. I believe this frame to be worth several times more than the extra cost, above the common non-reversible frame if we should never reverse it but once.

Again, I much prefer this frame to the old style, even if I never reversed it at all.

1. I am not troubled with sagging top-bars; and the outer bar, the one which governs the uniformity of the bee-space, or Langstroth shal-

low air-chamber below the honey-board, never sags. If the inner top-bar sags, it does little harm, and when reversed, the sag is thus corrected as it straightens back to place, and the new top-bar (just from the bottom) will not sag. In reversing, I either shake off the bees or revolve the inner frame very slowly.. I generally prefer to shake off the bulk of the bees, and I have found that on an average I spent five minutes to each hive (counting opening and closing) in performing the reversal of all the eight frames. Bits of comb and propolis bother but little, as the sharp corners of the wood pieces shave them away like a pair of shears.

2. It will be noticed in Fig. 1 that while the top and bottom bars of this frame position with the hive the same as other frames, the ends do not, and in this difference I find an improvement. It will also be noticed that the short end-piece is tapering, regarding its thickness. Now, as the whole end positions to the hive, the top is ¼ of an inch away from the hive end, the bottom of the short piece ⅜ of an inch, and all below that, ¾ of an inch away. This large opening, while it greatly facilitates the

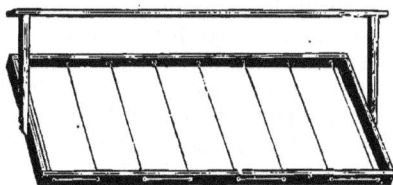

Fig. 2.

rapid and easy withdrawal or insertion of the frame, is in no way objectionable, as there is no danger of the bees building combs in even so large and handy a space where such space is no higher up than shown in the illustration.

While this frame is of slightly less surface capacity than the standard Langstroth frame, it has a greater brood capacity when reversed, and fits the same hive as the standard.

While I prefer this style of reversible frame, to any other, for Langstroth style of hives, I shall abandon it with the hive.

CHAPTER XXIV.

Our New Hive.

Many bee-keepers who have followed me in my past inventions, in trying to improve upon the Langstroth hive, and old system of management, and have adopted my new style of that hive, and of using it, and many of whom number their colonies by the hundred, may be surprised when they learn that I have been experimenting with, and have adopted an entirely different style of hive, and am at present supplanting the old with the new, in my own apiaries, numbering 450 colonies.

Since the time when Father Langstroth gave us his valuable inventions, much progress has been made in our chosen pursuit. His discoveries were so far in advance of his time, that while rapid and long strides have been made, in every other department of the pursuit, few, indeed, have been the improvements in hives. We have been able to improve upon some of the parts of his hive, but nearly all of the popular hives of to-day, embrace little else than his inventions. I think the same cannot be said of the new hive I am about to describe; a hive that after subjecting to practical tests, has become the decided choice, of all who have used it.

"Necessity is the mother of invention," it is said, and the great influx into the business of honey production, causing decline in prices, necessitates the use of such implements and methods—especially in hives—as will give us the greatest amount of surplus honey, for the amount of capital and labor invested.

Some of us have grown from boyhood to manhood, hand in hand with this pursuit, and while we are often complimented upon our thorough knowledge of the business, it is usually forgotten that we have as signally failed to become skilled in any other branch of industry. Such is the case, however, and after the best part of a life-time has been spent in any pursuit, when that pursuit languishes, circumstances tending to make it less profitable, the wise do not hastily desert it, adopting a stranger, but work the more persistently to counteract the detrimental influences, by bringing every possible advantage to bear upon the business. This has been our aim, in the invention of the New Hive. Only time can fully demonstrate to what extent we have succeeded in meeting this almost universal demand.

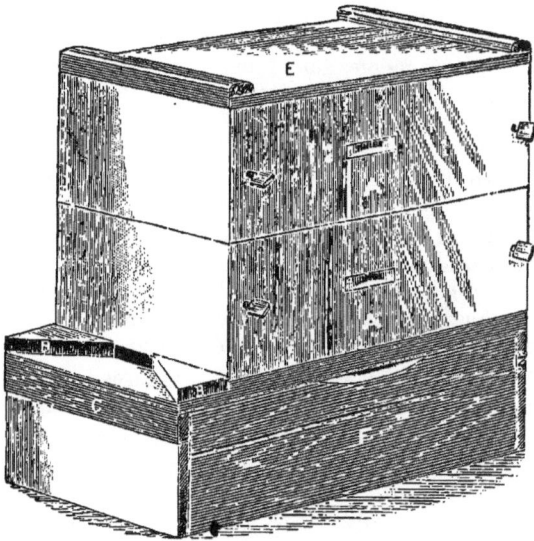

The above cut, though it makes the cases appear disproportionately high, will aid us in describing our New Hive; a hive which in many features, as well as its system of management, differs from anything of which I have ever seen or heard, although I have read nearly all of the books devoted to bee-culture, and have nearly every copy of all the periodicals ever published in the United States, upon the subject.

In viewing the cut, you will notice that the brood-chamber, as well as the surplus department, is composed of two or more

HORIZONTAL SECTIONS,

or departments, each containing a full set of eight frames, each department being not only "reversible," or, more properly termed, invertible, but each part perfectly interchangeable with every other.

After having enjoyed the immense advantages accruing from the Tiering system as applied to surplus cases, the idea came to my mind, that equal advantages could be realized from the application of the same principle, to the brood department.

But this is not all. In practicing the "contraction method," and trying to overcome its imperfections, while enjoying its many advantages, I was firmly impressed that it would give us much more perfectly and completely, the results desired, if we could make the contraction by taking away the top of the brood-chamber, rather than its sides.

Following up this suggestion, I determined to make a hive whose brood-chamber should be in two or more horizontal sections, or departments.

The question next arose, "what shall be the style, size and shape of these cases constituting the brood-chamber, and of what style, number and adjustment shall be their frames?"

After consulting the recorded experience of others, as well as my own, I determined to make each brood-chamber part, the same width and length as that of my old hive, using the same thickness of lumber for ends and sides, and make the depth such as would give each part the same comb capacity as is contained in five standard L. frames.

By careful computation, I found that my cases, to hold the frames, would need to be 5½ inches high, while the frames themselves would be bee-space less in depth, or 5⅜ inches, outside measure.

The next problem to be solved was, "what style of frame and frame adjustment, shall I use?" I pondered long upon this question. I was not forgetful of the many advantages peculiar to the "Laterally Movable Frames," nor of corresponding disadvantages of "Fixed Frames," as commonly used. I was mindful of the fact that each style of frame had its own peculiar advantages and disadvantages, and that many of us had decided that, all things considered, the Laterally Movable Frames gave us most advantages, though many of our most successful honey producers, among whom may be named T. F. Bingham, Chas. Dadant & Son, and the Hetheringtons, preferred and successfully used frames with closed end bars.

I had also learned the advantages accruing from "reversing" or inverting combs, and determined that, notwithstanding each section or part of my new brood-chamber complete with its 8 shallow frames, was reversible, and reversing each part with its frames, all together, would be the common practice, I would have each brood-frame separately reversible.

The result was that I adopted a plain, simple frame, with simple and practical adjustment, that not only gave the advantages desired, but by virtue of its shallowness, reversibleness and the valuable use of comb foundation for comb guides, removes nearly all the objectionable features resulting from the use of closed-end frames, at the same time giving us more than the usual advantages gained by their use, by virtue of the method of adjustment, and manner in which they are secured in proper position.

I will now proceed to describe the frames and method of adjustment in the case, which consists of one horizontal section or department of the brood-chamber. First, a brief description of the case, which is 13x19⅞x5⅜ inches, outside measure, the end pieces being of ⅞ and the side pieces of ¼ inch lumber (after being dressed on both sides), the long pieces being nailed to the short ones. Before nailing the pieces together, however, a rabbet is cut in each edge of each piece. Supposing the pieces to stand up edgewise, the rabbet is cut downward three-sixteenths of an inch and back from the inner side of the board ⅜ inch in the side pieces, and ½ inch in the end pieces, which leaves ⅝ inch of wood outside the rabbet on each of the four pieces.

The above cut, also imperfect, failing to show the rabbet in the top edge of the cases, will perhaps aid the reader to better understand my description.

After the four pieces are nailed together and form the case, we nail a strip of tin, ⅝ inch wide and 12 inches long, down snugly into the rabbet on one and the same edge of each of the end pieces. You will see that this strip of tin projects inward into the case ⅛ inch. and is up from what we will now call the bottom edge, three-sixteenths of an inch. We now have two small strips of wood ¼x⅜x5⅜, which we nail in the corners of the case, onto one of the side pieces, the ⅜ side down, and centrally located in the case, as regards the top and bottom. These cleats are called "offsets;" they are not new, and not essentially a part of my invention.

In the opposite side of the case, centrally located up and down, as close to the end of the side pieces as will cause the hole to come through just close along beside the end pieces, we bore two ⅝ holes, and cut a thread in them, turning in a wood thumb-screw (See cut). The eight little openings at the corners are filled with small blocks, tacked in. Now the case is complete.

Our brood frames are made as follows: The end pieces are ⅜x1⅜x5⅝. Top and bottom-bars ¼x13-16x18 1-16. They are "dovetailed," or notched at the corners, like surplus section boxes, so that when driven together, their exact outside measure is 5⅝x18 1-16, while their case is 5¾x18⅛, inside measure.

When dropped down onto the tin rests, they fit the case loosely by 1-16 of an inch in length, and position so as to leave 3-16, or one-half bee space, above and below their top and bottom bars, which are just alike.

In other words, they are centrally located within the case, which being bee space deeper than the frames, leaves just one-half bee space above, and the same below them.

It will be seen that the end pieces of these frames are 9-16 wider than the tops and bottoms, hence the spaces between the top and bottom-bars will always be 9-16 of an inch. When the 8 frames are in position in the case, turn up the thumb-screws, and by virtue of the "offsets" and these screws, the end pieces of both outside frames will be held ¼ inch from the sides of the case, which leaves the same space between the top bars of the outside frames and the sides of the case, that exists between the top bars themselves, which gives the bees a chance and directs them to make the outside combs of the same thickness of the others.

The reader will also see that the tops and bottoms of the frames come just even with the rabbets in the edges of all the pieces that form the cases, and that wherever said cases find a resting place, they have a bearing of but ⅜ inch, all around. After once using hive-stories, or cases, that have such narrow bearings, I predict that no one would be persuaded to return to the old seven-eights bearings. With the ⅜ bearing, one can adjust stories to the bottom board, or to each other, in less than one-half the time usually required, and with far less liability of crushing bees. This important advantage is the only reason for all the rabbets, except the two that hold the tin rests. Our

BOTTOM-BOARD,

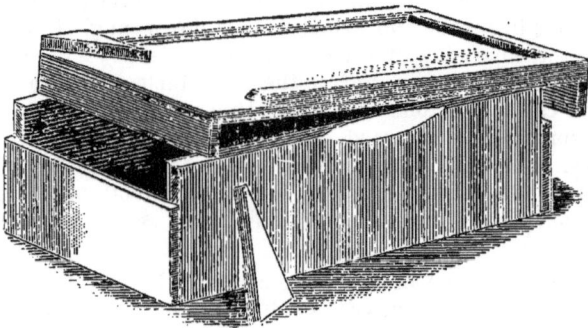

you will notice, is made almost exactly like our old one, except that it is not fast to the hive, but complete within itself. We take the same board that we use for the bottom of the old hive, viz: 13x22½x⅞. and cleat it at each extreme end with cleats 13x1½x⅞, nailed edgewise to the bottom-board. By observing the cut, you will see how the bottom-stand is made, and how the bottom-board fits the same. The cleats of the bottom-board touch the narrower end pieces of the bottom-stand, just a trifle before the bottom-board proper, touches its wider side pieces. Such a bearing causes the weight of the hive to assist the cleats in always keeping the bottom-board perfectly straight.

You will also notice that the upper surface of the bottom-board is provided with cleats, which are tacked to it in such manner as to form a large bee space of over ¼ inch, under the brood frames and over the bottom-board. The two side cleats are just 19⅝ inches long, and are beveled, so that their top surface is ¾ wide, and their lower surface ⅜ wide, and they are ⅜ high. The object of the bevel is to give them a very solid bearing.

The cut will show you that they are nailed on flush with the back end, and are just as long as the hive. Another cleat of the same pattern, and proper length, runs across the back end, between the two side cleats.

You will observe the hand-holds in the cases, as well as the place cut away in the bottom-stand, which admits of a sure and quick grasp of the bottom-board, when desired to remove it with the hive. The

HONEY-BOARD,

with the new hive, is made just like our old one (see cuts), except that instead of having its bee space all on one side, it is one-half on each side, and a honey board thus constructed is stronger than any other. The queen excluding metal, works into these one-half bee-space honey-boards most admirably, and for all I can see at present, we had better use the metal, when we use queen excluding honey-boards. We may be able to make wood answer for queen excluding, but as yet, all have failed to do so, satisfactorily. The

COVER

is of the same outside dimensions as the hive; is of ⅜ lumber, cleated with ⅜ cleats. and small cleats ⅜x3-16 are tacked all around its lower extreme outer edge, so that it, too, has a one-half bee space in its under side. You will now see that all the cases and the honey-board, each contain a one-half bee-space on each side, and consequently are perfectly reversible at will, without adding to, or taking anything from them; simply turn them over. The bottom board and cover could also have been constructed to reverse, or invert, but not to any advantage that would have compensated for the necessary loss of a greater durability and other advantages gained by its present construction. I need say nothing of the

SURPLUS CASES,

further than that they are constructed on the same plan as are the brood-chamber cases, just described. They are proper depth for receiving a wide-frame, constructed just like the brood frame described, except with top, bottom and end bars, whose widths exactly correspond with the widths of the top, bottom and end pieces of the 7 to the foot sections, mentioned on page 63.

Each surplus case is also invertible at will, like the brood cases. having the screws to hold the wide-frames fast, and is as properly one side up as the other.

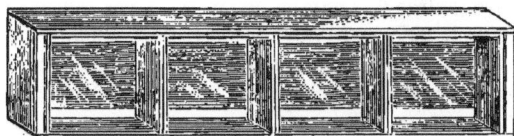

Above is illustrated the style of the wide-frame, showing how the sections are adjusted within it. This cut is also imperfect, making the frame appear the same width all around, while really the top and bottom are ⅜ inch narrower than the end pieces. Our surplus case receives seven of them at once, holding a tier of 28 sections. Each wide-frame is supplied with a tin separator in the ordinary way, as shown in the cut.

These wide-frames are also notched at their corners, the same as are the brood frames, and after they are driven together, we tack on our tin separators in a most perfectly taut manner, as follows:

Lay the frame on a board, with cleats tacked to the same, to guide the frame to a true square. Now spring inward, the top and bottom bars, which tends to slightly shorten the frame. Now tack on the separator, and when the frame is removed. it will forever hold it true, and the tin will be taut as a drum head.

These wide-frame-cases are one story high, and are worked upon the Tiering-up system. They are the same length as the brood cases; the ends are rabbeted the same, to receive the tin rests, and narrow the resting surface; but their width is greater than the width of the brood cases, except at their edges, which are the same, by virtue of an outside bevel, which also narrows their ⅝ sides to the regular ⅝ rest.

The cover fits the honey board, surplus and brood cases, all equally perfect. The thumb-screws turn up very easily and quickly, and their power is so much greater than one might imagine, that when set against the frames, if the case be inverted, so as to lose all use of the tin rests, the screws prove ten times sufficient. The tins are used to hold the frames to proper position when adjusting them to the case, or removing them for overhauling the brood department, for minute inspection.

Although these are "fixed frames," they are readily removed, by simply loosening the screws. I will endeavor to explain how we overcome the usual difficulties accompanying such frames. By virtue of the exceeding shallowness of our frames, and the use of comb foundation, we procure combs almost perfectly straight. The greatest trouble usually arises from uneven combs—combs irregular at their tops, just above the cells occupied with brood. This occurs mainly from the fact that where bees use combs for storing, they leave only about ¼ inch space between them, while those used for brood are about twice that distance apart. These shallow frames, and the practice of inverting and interchanging the cases containing them, gives us straight, uniform combs throughout, and completely filled with brood nearly all the time when we manipulate them.

Among the important advantages of this peculiarly constructed brood chamber is the one of perfect

INTERCHANGEABLENESS

of all its horizontal cases, or parts.

The reader will remember at just what time in the year we used eight combs, and at what time five combs, in our L. hives, when practicing the contraction method. You will now observe that when we use one brood case only, we are contracted to an equivalent of five L. combs, and when we use two such cases, we are giving brooding space equal to ten L. combs, and so on.

Now we use in our brood department one case, or two cases, at the same time we are using five combs, or eight combs, with the old hive, when practicing contraction. The new hive and its system of management is a great improvement over the old, for the following reasons:

1st. When contracting the new brood-chamber, we divide it horizontally, instead of vertically, taking away its top, rather than sides, giving us all the advantages of a very shallow hive, with brood close up to the top bars, and directly under all parts of the surplus case. This extremely shallow brood department settles the brace-comb problem, as with it, the bees will build scarcely any of these braces, on the tops of the upper bars of such shallow frames.

2nd. We make the change from the capacity of the ten L. frame hive, to five L. frames, almost instantaneously, and without exposure to robbers should there be any abroad.

3rd. When enlarging, by adding to the brood department (when the queen needs more room in spring) by the new method we not only perform the work thus quickly, but we place the empty case of combs under the case of brood; and while downward is the natural direction in which the queen tends to spread her brood nest, upward is the direction taken by heat, and this settles the question of "danger in spreading brood," should the temperature suddenly fall. Although we have made an addition· to our brood-chamber which doubles its capacity and places the empty combs just where the queen will most readily occupy them, we have spread no brood.

Regarding the advantages of shallow combs, let me extract from Father Langstroth's article in the American Bee Journal for 1883, page 490:

"The broad and low shape, in addition to giving the much desired top surface for surplus honey receptacles, has the following advantages:

It is obviously much better adapted to the use of upper stories, than taller hives. It seems more natural to bees to place their stores over their central brood-nest, than anywhere else. Why should bees attempt the difficult work of upward comb building, against the law of gravity, by which their suspended combs are kept in a perpendicular position, while they have ample side room for building them in the natural way? Why, I say, do they act thus, unless it is most in accordance with their instincts to place their stores above their brood-nest?

If honey, to have its choicest flavor, ought not to be extracted—as the Dadants and other of our leading apiarists assert—before it has been capped, and if when all bee-work is most pressing, more colonies can be taken care of by piling hive upon hive, filled with empty combs—to be emptied when more leisure comes—then the advantages of shallow hives are easy to be seen.

Long and shallow frames are more convenient for most of our necessary manipulations.

In handling them the arms take a natural and easy, instead of a cramped position.

With such frames the eye commands the whole surface of a comb, in searching for the queen, etc., without that uncomfortable craning of the neck which deep frames compel.

As has been already explained, there is less danger of hurting bees in removing or replacing the shallow frames.

Less motion, and of course less time, is needed to take out or put back such frames."

While years of practical experience has taught me the truthfulness of the above statements, together with other important advantages accruing from the use of shallow frames, I have also become firmly convinced that the very shallowest combs used by any of us, are just as safe upon which to winter our colonies. If you will consult Mr. Bingham, who for more than a quarter of a century has continually used a brood-chamber containing eight combs, whose length is all of 22 inches, and depth but 4½ and 5 inches; using these hives beside others of all depths, I think he will tell you that the idea that shallow combs are not as well adapted to safely wintering their colonies, as deeper ones, is one of the greatest mistakes of bee-keepers.

My experience of 17 winters with the use of combs, varying in depth from 4½ to 20 inches, stands in favor of the shallow combs, for wintering; accidentally so, I believe, however, for I feel quite sure that the wintering problem does not hinge upon the depth of the combs employed, and that it has little or nothing to do with it.

In the past extremely severe winter, during the great mortality in other apiaries as well as my own, when I lost three-fourths of my colonies, one in the long shallow combs (whose depth is but 4½ inches) came through the trying ordeal, proving to be the strongest colony in my yard, with one exception. This colony was wintered out-doors with one-half the thickness of packing used about the others. I have wintered in these. combs, out-doors, thus packed. eight winters, and lost but once, which is better than the average of my apiaries during that time. Though in my latitude, I shall adhere to cellar wintering. with any hive, were I intending to leave my colonies on their summer. stands, I should employ but one brood case of the new hive, for the purpose.

If, however, others may differ with me, preferring hives even deeper than the standard Langstroth, if they will use two brood cases they will have just such a hive; the bee-space between the two sets of frames serving as winter passage-ways through and among the combs. It becomes obvious that the brood department of this hive can be made in one story, of any length, breadth or depth, preferred; and while losing the advantages of tiering and interchanging in the brood department, the other advantages enumerated, may be enjoyed.

Having the brood-chamber in two horizontal sections, or parts, admitting of interchanging the upper with the lower portion, at will, for the purposes specified, placing the part containing the most honey, below, putting both in a new position. produces many of the same results and advantages given us by inverting, and is made complete by reversing one or both of the parts, as their condition may direct, when making the interchange.

The system of interchanging, admits of using more than two sets of the frames in the brood department, if any should so desire, and whatever number is used, it enables the bee-master to keep his surplus cases and honey-board, always next to his brood.

After three years of careful experimenting, I much prefer to have my brood-chamber no larger than two cases at any time of year, and no larger than one case after the colony swarms, till up to the time the queen's capacity is equal to more room, the following spring; a time when the use of such capacity will give us strong colonies for surplus storing. I have found the advantages of contracted brood-chambers to be so great, that I much prefer to use them at all times when a greater laying capacity given the queen, is of no special value.

Let us return to the subject of surplus cases, and discuss for a moment the question of wide-frames and separators, vs. section cases. As before stated in this chapter, I think that the light section case, generally known as "Heddon's Case," is the best non-separator case extant, and I believe such is generally admitted. These cases, made to hold surplus section boxes without frames or separators, have become popular with practical honey producers, who, before adopting and testing them, had used wide-frames and separators. In every case that has come to my knowledge, however, the wide-frames used by the gentlemen mentioned, were two-story; i. e., deep enough to hold two tiers of 4½ sections; two separators being attached to each frame. These frames, as well as the cases containing them, were heavy and bungling, their shape illy adapting them to fit each other or be keyed up snugly together. This was not all: The worst feature regarding these two-story supers, was that they were not at all adapted to the tiering method, and invited the bees to commence their surplus work too far from the brood.

During the past four seasons, while using many of my favorite non-separatored cases, I have also used by their side several hundred one-story wide-frame cases, with separators, and have become a convert to them. I know that each style of case possesses advantages over the other, and I feel certain that any practical honey producer who will thoroughly test my new style of wide-frame case, will agree with me that it is, every-thing considered, the best of all.

It is not only equally well adapted to the tiering method, but is con-structed so that all its separators are straight and taut; so that its frames are at all times pressed so tightly that no room is left for propolis, or bee-glue, and otherwise arranged to avoid gluing; slip out of the cases all in a body, when the screws are loosened. Thus we have reserved all the ad-vantages of wide-frames and separators, at the same time discarding nearly all their disadvantages.

The above is reason enough for changing our preference, but that is not all. This style of surplus case is alone eminently adapted to

REVERSING SECTIONS.

For two years we have been testing the practice of reversing our sur-plus section boxes. As one might guess, the same law which governs the operations of bees when their brood combs are reversed, or inverted, equally applies to their actions when reversing their surplus combs.

If you watch the progress in a surplus case, and when you find the least developed comb is worked out to that extent that it has a firm, broad bearing on the top piece, and its sides are attached to the side pieces of the section. at least part way down, if you now invert the surplus case with all its contents, work will go speedily forward; for inverting hastens cap-ping, and when the combs are completed, they are not only beautiful to behold, and most substantial to ship, but allow the purchaser to notice no objectionable tare. The section itself becomes almost obscured, as it were. Their shipping qualities, however, are of greatest importance.

It sometimes happens, especially when honey is coming in more slowly, that the bees will taper off and completely cap over some of the surplus combs before they have built others to sufficient size to bear inverting without great danger of lopping over sidewise.

These differences are confined to different positions, reckoned side-wise in the case, and it is usually the sections in the outside wide-frames which are behind in development.

Notwithstanding my new cases can be reversed and as properly ad-justed, with a single motion, each wide-frame is also perfectly invertable, and in the few cases in which we have found this slow development in the two outside frames, we have quickly loosened the screws, inverted thsee two frames, again turned up the screws, then inverted the whole case, leaving these outside combs again as we found them, with the others all inverted.

A word in regard to the cause of bees neglecting their outside surplus combs, as compared to their work upon the others.

If the reader has ever constructed a hive whose surplus department was wider than the brood-chamber, jutting out over the same, he has noticed the partial neglect paid by the bees, to the surplus boxes which rested over wood, instead of comb.

Now this same difference made by the bees, between wood and comb, they will also make between combs of honey and combs of brood, and with our 8 frame L. hive, we notice far less of this neglect of the side surplus combs, than we noticed when using 10 frame hives. This is one objection to the method of contracting by replacing the side combs of L. brood-chambers with fillers or dummies; with the new hive, however, the method of contraction is such that all the combs of the brood-chamber are filled with brood.

We have constructed this hive for reversing, in two different ways; the one described in the preceding pages, and as follows, either carrying out the principles upon which our invention is based.

In the first that we made we cut no rabbets in the edges of the cases, using them with full width bearings, and we tacked the tin rests or stops, at the extreme bottom of the case. The frames rested flush with one side of the case, and full bee-space below the other. The cover was flat, i. e., without containing any half bee-space; the honey-board of the old style, flat on one side and full bee-space on the other, and the cleats on the bottom-board $\frac{1}{2}$ inch higher.

After inverting a case, we had to loosen its thumb-screws, and placing it crosswise of the lower case, or bottom-board, push the frames through to the other side, again tightening the screws.

Notwithstanding I devised both methods at nearly the same time, I first chose this latter one, because it admitted of using the old cover, honey-board, and old style of non-reversible cases, greatly favoring those who had many of them on hand. After more experience, however, I changed my choice to the plan first described and illustrated by the cuts, which I now very much prefer, and expect to use exclusively in the future.

To adjust one of our old cases to the new hive, we only have to make a honey-board with a half bee-space on one side, and whole bee-space on the other; or we can use the new honey-board by building up one side to a full bee-space, by tacking on strips of proper width and $\frac{1}{8}$ inch in thickness.

Bees can pass through our one-half bee-space of three-sixteenths of an inch, but we would not advise so small a space for general use, because it will be more readily filled with comb and propolis. I presume the reader understands that whether the brood or surplus department consists, one or both, of one or more cases, the honey-board is always kept between the two departments.

While introducing our old style hive to the public, we have many times been asked if there was not danger of the cases being blown off, and rain leaking in, where stories did not over-lap, but simply rested flat upon each other, touching only at their edges.

I will here answer by saying that, although we have so used them for years, and during that time sold thousands of these hives to others, we have neither experienced, nor received reports of any such trouble.

Hive-stories, to handle easily, should at once admit of a lateral movement, which "telescoping" stories will not do. I look upon this point as a very important one, in the proper construction of hives.

GENERAL MANAGEMENT.

I will endeavor to outline the system of management, to which the New Hive is adapted; a system that it is believed, will give us the best results, with the greatest economy of time and labor. Before going further, I will quote again from Mr. Hutchinson, in the "Country Gentleman," as evidence of the fact that our brightest producers will welcome just such a hive and system as the one we are describing:

"The thought and energy of the whole bee-keeping world appears to be directed toward the invention of a reversible frame. Strange as it may appear, scarcely any thought is given toward the invention of a reversible hive. It is the writer's opinion that this idea of reversal will yet develop a reversible hive; it will not stop with a reversible frame. It is, perhaps, natural that invention should progress step by step, but when the advantages of a reversible hive over a reversible frame are so obvious, it is really deplorable that so much should be wasted upon an intermediate step. It is possible that bee-keepers are so backward in this because they know that the adoption of a reversible hive would necessitate the casting aside of the hives now in use. Perhaps another reason is, that a reversible hive will require a different style of frame from the ordinary hanging one, and bee-keepers argue that this style of frame must be preserved, because it is so much more easily handled. Those who have been following this line of thought would do well to consider whether the time is not near at hand when hives, not frames, will be manipulated.

A beginner in bee-keeping always handles the combs of the brood-nest more than does the veteran. Until he opens the hive and makes an examination, he cannot tell whether there is a queen in the hive, whether she is laying, whether honey is coming in, or whether the bees are starving; while the practiced bee-keeper, like the experienced physician, can judge of internal conditions by observing external symptoms. Many of our most successful apiarists do not disturb the brood-nest from one year's end to the other. The Heddon method of preventing after-swarming is an illustration of how we shall yet learn to manage bees by manipulating hives instead of frames. It is not necessary or advisable in making a reversible hive, or in so managing bees as to avoid handling the combs, that movable combs be discarded, as there are times, when a colony is queenless, or short of stores, or something of that sort, when movable combs are a great convenience; but to think that combs must be moved, all through the working season, simply because they can be moved, is a wrong idea.

When we have learned to manage an apiary by means of "movable hives" (?) then the work of raising honey will be much nearer automatic, and it will be more profitable for experienced apiarists to establish out apiaries. When this time arrives, and the successful wintering of bees has become an established fact, bee-keeping will become more of a specialty than ever."

The above perfectly illustrates many of the basic truths underlying the superiority of the system of management connected with this hive. One year ago, I was visiting a well known and justly celebrated honey producer, and while overlooking his fine, large apiary, he remarked as follows:

"In those three back rows, there are forty-five hives in excellent condition, not one of which have been opened in five years."

At that date the hives consisted of the brood-chambers only, and it was of them that he spoke. Those colonies were managed for surplus only, and worked by a bee-master of twenty years' experience, and had, I think, yielded a larger profit on the capital and labor expended, than any equal number of colonies in the country. Here we have practical experience similar to my own, verifying the statements made by Mr Hutchinson. I have no doubt but that many important manipulations were made with those forty-five hives, but none of the purposes of these manipulations necessitated moving the frames. No favors were ever shown robbers. Very little time was employed for any manipulation.

I have so constructed the New Hive, that natural swarms can be hived, increase made artificially, queen cells all cut out, queens found, or their laying determined, the combs almost or quite cleared of all bees, queens or cells introduced, brood-chambers contracted or enlarged, combs all inverted, prime swarms prevented or discouraged, after-swarming prevented, and many other useful manipulations performed in less than one-fourth the time usually employed, because we do it all without the necessity of handling the frames.

It is true that the special comb honey producer, even with this hive, will, in rare instances, need to move the brood-frames, and when he does, he will find them among the very easiest of removal and re-adjustment. They are combs of brood, not honey. He will find that in their removal from, and replacing in, the case, their arrangement with each other and the case, reduces the danger of crushing bees, or the pains needed to prevent the same, to the minimum. You will remember that the frames are only about five inches deep, outside measure, and the top and bottom pieces just the width of the thickness of worker brood combs. Also that the ends of the frames fit each other, and the ends of the case snugly. Bees cannot go between or behind them.

After a case has been inverted, you will find the combs built out solid in these frames. There will then be no ledges, or open places in which bees can lodge. There will be only nine straight ranges between the eight combs and sides of the case. These openings will be a little over one-half inch in width.

Suppose now that we are approaching our hive, and wish to find the queen. We puff a small volume of smoke across the entrance, to drive in and subdue the guards; lift the cover, blow a whiff of smoke down into the surplus case, or cases. Now lift them with the honey-board, from the brood-case, pour a volume of smoke onto the top of the brood-frames, and wait a moment, and usually by lifting the case you will see your queen on the bottom-board. When she fails to run down, puff once more upon the tops of the frames and shake your case over a shade-board, in front of the hive, and your queen and nearly every bee will be found on that board. We have done this on very many occasions, and always with the same results; and we do the work in less time than you have taken to read our description of procedure.

If we wish to clip queen-cells (something we do not practice), we pick up our case, shake out the bees, and standing the case on end, we can see every cell from one side or the other, and cut out every one with a common pocket-knife, and do it in less time than we can get out the first frame from our common hives, in many instances.

As we can, almost with a motion, divest a case of practically all of its bees, and the cases being so shallow and comb spaces equally open on each side, you will perceive with what ease and dispatch we can perform nearly every necessary manipulation. During the short period that we employ two brood-cases, we sometimes have to handle the second one to complete our work.

For shade, during the heated season, we use a board two feet wide and three feet long. These we sometimes cut from wide boards, but oftener form them by cleating two or more boards together. Our hives front east, and the shade-boards rest lengthwise on the hive, about centrally situated, but sidewise we place the north edge of the board even with the north side of the hive, allowing all its extra width to project over on the south, or sunny side. This board shades the hive, except in early morn, and just before sunset. We hold the shade-board in place by the use of a stone weighing about fifteen pounds, and we find that we can handle this stone with ease. and very much quicker than we could manipulate hooks or other devices to hold the board in place.

Our surplus registers being always on the north side of the cases, are never obscured by this shade-board.

Among other important advantages gained by this system of manipulation, I wish to call the reader's attention to three: The sudden admission of light from both sides of the case (an admission which is complete, owing to the shallowness of the combs, and wide opening between them) is almost equal to smoke, in its tendency to subdue the bees.

Again: the practical bee-keeper has observed how immediately bees willingly yield to manipulation, giving up all attempts to protect their stores, when suddenly shaken from their combs. The bees that attack us, are usually from the combs not yet shaken. With our system we pinch no bees, nor otherwise irritate them; and when we shake them from the case, they at once give up all ideas of opposition, lying quiet, and completely subdued.

Another no less important feature connected with the system, is the very slight exposure of the combs to robbers, during any ordinary manipulation. Since the introduction of our surplus cases and one-story wide-frame supers, we have been able to remove them, and shake out nearly all the bees, without exposure to robbers. Now. we have gained much of the same advantages, as applied to the brood department.

Years ago, I learned that for ease and effectiveness in dislodging the foothold of bees, whether shaking them from a single frame of comb, or out of a case, a trembling, vibratory motion, added to an easy, jerking movement, was the best.

If you have carefully followed our description of how we work our old style of hive, for comb honey, on the contraction and tiering system, you now understand how we manage the New Hive for the same results. We have also shown how we can accomplish many desired ends, by the tiering of brood and surplus departments, and how we can accomplish nearly all that is desirable, by handling cases, rather than frames.

You can now-guess how well adapted and easy of manipulation is the New Hive

FOR EXTRACTED HONEY.

For this purpose we supply ourselves with an ample number of brood cases, for each colony. After deciding how many of these cases we wish to devote to breeding, and how many to surplus honey, we place a queen-excluding honey-board, as before described, between the cases devoted to the different purposes. We produce the very best of extracted honey in these shallow cases by the tiering-up method, as described by Mr. Dadant in his able little work on "Extracted Honey," and practiced by ourselves over twelve years ago, with shallow L. frame supers, used upon full depth hives, upon the same tiering plan.

By years of experience, we well know the superiority of this method of raising extracted honey for sweet sauce. When using the L. frames exclusively, and shipping most of my extracted honey to manufacturers, to save complication regarding size of frames, I preferred one story of the same size frames, for my surplus department; but now there is no sale for "unripe" honey, and as I am choosing shallow frames for my brood-cases, I certainly again advise, and shall practice using all frames alike, and upon the tiering system, to which these frames are so well adapted. When extracting, the bees can be removed from the cases by shaking, and all the frames removed from the case at once, by laying it upon our honey table, and loosening the thumb-screws, when the case can be lifted from all the combs, with a single motion.

When commencing the use of this style of hive for extracting, as with others it becomes necessary, of course, to have combs built in your frames; a work which we greatly facilitate by the use of comb founda-tion. We wire these little frames with No. 30 plated wire, and fill them with full sheets of foundation, the same as we have done with the L. frames, as described on pages 62 and 63. As our top-bars are quite thin, (for which there are good reasons) we place between them in central po-sition and pressed into one side of the foundation, the slim metal stand-ard which has been used in L. frames for some years, which was given to the public, I believe, by Mr. Root, of Medina.

You will see that our extracting cases are precisely like the brood-cases, and can at any time be used for either purpose; or in other words, we use a series of brood-cases for extracting purposes, worked upon the tiering plan, using queen excluding honey-boards to limit the queen to any given number, according to the season; or she may be allowed to range at will through all the cases, as has been the former practice; which, while it has a tendency to discourage swarming, it can by no means be depended upon to entirely prevent it in my location, consequently I much prefer to confine the queen to one or two cases, much the same as we do when producing comb honey.

In locations similar to my own, where we have an autumn harvest consisting of amber-colored honey, which brings very nearly as much in the extracted form as in combs, I have found it advisable, even with the old style of hive, to prepare them a double outfit of surplus receptacles; one for comb honey, as before described, and another consisting of eight regular L. combs in a super of the same size of the brood-chamber. At the close of the white honey harvest, all receptacles for comb honey would be removed, the extracting supers taking their place for securing the fall crop.

With the new style of hive, we use the extra brood-cases in the same way and at the same time we formerly used the old extracting supers. While I practice hiving swarms upon foundation, in one of the brood-cases, with one or two section cases above, when I wish to add a second case to this colony, the following spring, I much prefer to have combs, rather than foundation, and these we will have on hand, having had them drawn during the preceding fall harvest.

Without consuming space in giving the reasons, I think the reader now understands the construction and method of manipulation connected with this hive, sufficiently to realize its adaptability to queen-rearing, and hiving second swarms whenever the bee-keeper desires rapid increase.

In the preceding chapter we spoke of contraction as a means of bringing the brood-chamber at the close of honey gathering, out in an almost honeyless condition, which placed the same amount of honey in the surplus receptacles that otherwise would have been in the brood combs.

The reader will not fail to realize that this contraction, when practiced with the New Hive, will more perfectly accomplish that desired end. He will also see how well adapted is this arrangement, to wintering his bees upon natural stores, without feeding at all: for he can at any time during the season and during the honey flow from any variety of blossoms whose nectar he may consider safest for winter stores, quickly fill a brood-case of combs with said preferred honey, laying the same away until just at the close of brood-rearing, when he can transfer the bees into it in one minute by placing it upon their stand and shaking them all out of their case, letting them run into the new one; or it may be placed on top of the old one, and most of the bees be driven up into it with smoke, the remainder being shaken from the old case as before, or the old case may be left under the full one throughout the winter, if they are to be wintered on the summer stand, and the bee-keeper fancies they will be safer with greater comb depth. In either case the stores will be always accessible.

I think the reader will plainly see that this arrangement for a bee-hive, is most eminently adapted to the speedy accomplishment of almost any desired end pertaining to the winter or summer management of bees.

Although we gain most profit from the production of light honey, by selling it in the comb, we have not failed to realize that during our most copious honey flows we meet with loss that the extracted honey producer does not suffer, from the fact that our wax-working bees cannot construct combs fast enough to furnish storage room for the field workers.

Many have endeavored to overcome this loss by extracting from their brood-chambers, which have usually heretofore been so large that much of their comb capacity has been occupied with honey representing idle capital. It proved, however, that such a practice only tended to change our crop of honey from comb, to the extracted form, as the bees immediately re-filled the empty combs before the queen could occupy them.

and if the bee-master again extracted them, again they would be re-filled, the bees at the same time, more or less withdrawing their forces from the surplus department; thus their efforts to prevent the loss, were futile. The arrangement of the New Hive is perfectly adapted to overcoming this difficulty.

When our basswood blossoms begin to secrete nectar in quantities beyond the capacity of our comb builders, we place a brood section of empty combs on top of our surplus cases, all being interchangeable and perfectly fitting each other. The completed storage room given in this position, catches the overflow, and at the same time does not discourage the completion of the surplus section combs, as does extracting from the brood-chamber. This brood, or extracting case, can be removed at any stage of its development preferred by the bee-keeper (we usually leave it till about one-half of the cells are capped over), then taken to the honey-house and extracted at once if the combs are needed, or placed on end with sides left open, in which there is no better place off the hives for honey to "ripen" to its most perfect consistency.

Though we have never made or used such, we think an extractor should be constructed to take eight of these shallow frames at once. They should rest lengthwise in a vertical position, hanging by the projection of one of their end bars, the lower projection passing under the wire frame rest, and all can be turned around without lifting out of the machine.

These shallow combs contain many less hollows, or sunken places, which greatly facilitates the uncapping process.

This fact and others which favor their adaptability to the extractor, we think more than overcomes the disadvantage resulting from the greater number to handle.

I believe that by virtue of the style and method of adjustment of the bottom-board, cases and honey-board, that by using the latter, made queen-excluding, we can place them in such way as to control swarming, and flight of drones, without the serious objections realized by the use of entrance attachments, which we have enumerated on pages 22 and 23.

If you place one of the queen-excluding honey-boards on the bottom-board, and the brood cases upon it, you will preserve proper bee-spaces throughout, and force all bees to pass through the honey-board, in leaving or entering the hive. The drones and queen cannot leave or enter the cases. By experiment we found that this arrangement did not retard ventilation, nor in any way disturb the normal tranquility of the colony; but farther than this, we have not experimented. What shall we do with our imprisoned drones? How can we catch our queens, when they attempt to go out with the swarms?

I have faith in a simple arrangement, for catching and holding them imprisoned, in a movable box, adjusted to the side of the brood-chamber, near the front end, but not in front of the entrance; thus in no way retarding ventilation, or egress and ingress of the workers. As soon as perfected and tested, it will be publicly described, and attached to the New Hive, if proven a practical success.

Although of plain and simple construction, I have not in the foregoing, aimed to give a detailed description of the New Hive; one intended to guide to accurately manufacturing the same.

Had I endeavored to do so, I should have failed to impart all the knowledge required to warrant all of our bee-keepers, who might so desire, in attempting to construct the hive, perfect in all its essential features. The only safe guide—the only one upon which I wish to place its reputation—is a complete and perfect sample to work from.

I have endeavored to describe the hive and system of manipulation adapted to it, sufficiently to impart to my readers, in so far as possible, that same knowledge of its superiority, that is possessed by myself and the few others who have practically tested it.

I trust that nearly all of my readers now comprehend the ease, comfort and dispatch with which an apiary can be managed to a dollar and cent success, with all its colonies in our new style of hive.

I trust that you realize the many advantages that always belonged to all styles of "fixed frames," and that in the arrangement of this hive, nearly all of their former disadvantages have been obviated.

The depth of the cases is such that six inch pine lumber, if it runs full width and is dry, will be suitable for their construction. This is no small item, as pine of that width can be purchased of much better quality, at the same price of wider lumber.

The construction of this hive is not adapted to inaccurate work; all parts should be well made, of good material, and exact measurements.

The hive and method of management is so peculiar, and different from all others, that I do not predict for it a very easy or rapid introduction. Experience has taught me that the advantages realized in its practical use, are far greater than will be conceived by the theorizing of our most practical honey producers.

Last season I employed a bright apiarist, of many years' experience, to assist us for a few weeks during the rush of storing and queen-rearing. The first day in the apiary, he curiously looked over and handled some of the New Hives. He shook his head, and remarked: "I do not like your New Hive." A week later, he said: "I have handled several of your New Hives to-day, and I like them pretty well; much better than I thought I should." A few days passed, and said he: "I have come to like your New Hives better than anything I ever handled before." Nearly a week passed again, when one evening, sitting on our veranda, after supper, talking of other subjects, after a silence of some minutes, he looked down to the ground in a reflective manner, and said what I hope may prove true: "To-day I have handled many of your New Hives, and I am now forced to the conclusion that they are destined to revolutionize the production of comb honey."

I have no fears but that time and experience will cause bee-keepers to give it all the credit that belongs to it, and further than this, I should not and do not desire.

I have procured a patent upon the New Hive, and in the chapter on the subject of "patents," may be found my reasons for so doing. I have been encouraged to do so by many of the best men of our brotherhood.

In a private letter, dated Sept. 30th, 1885, Father Langstroth pens the following, which I publish by his permission:

"He who makes an important invention and patents it, is a public benefactor, and no one who calls himself an honest man, should attempt to infringe upon his rights."

But for the occasional dishonest bee-keeper, no patent would be necessary; but I believe that the final interest of the great mass of honorable apiarists, as well as that of my own, demands the expense and trouble of the patent referred to.

Mr. Hutchinson, who, during the past season, thoroughly tested the New Hive, writes me that he finds it greatly superior to anything he has hitherto used, and now expects to use it to the exclusion of all other hives, in the future.

I do not claim perfection for this hive. After all my study and experimenting, it may still be open for improvement. I doubt, however, if any hive can be made, that will be equally good, unless it embraces some of its essential features.

In these chapters on hives, I have, in keeping with the spirit of this book, outlined only such construction and manipulation as I have found to be best. I have not aimed to discuss the merits and faults of implements and methods that I consider inferior. I have written from the standpoint of my own observation and experience.

CHAPTER XXV.

Wintering.

Have we yet found a satisfactory solution to this problem? I do not know just how to answer such a question. If it is a fact that we can carry safely through the winter and spring, any or all of our colonies, with as great certainty as we can winter our cows and horses, does that warrant us in answering the question in the affirmative? If so, I will say "yes."

But it still remains a fact, that while we have learned how to accomplish the above, we do not yet know just where the line may be drawn, between all the conditions that are, and that are not, necessary to the attainment of that very desirable result.

My past experiments compel the belief that I can winter my colonies with certainty, but just how to do so with the least trouble and expense, still remains an important problem for future experiments.

I feel positive that if I take a normal colony of bees, after all storing from natural sources is over, and exchange their combs for those containing neither pollen nor honey, and then feed them with a sufficient amount of properly prepared sugar syrup, place them in a cellar early, and keep the temperature at the proper point, their safe wintering becomes a practical certainty; but I am of the opinion that almost as good results can be attained, with less trouble; results of greater value, in proportion to their cost. The verification or disproval of the correctness of this opinion will be sought in my future experiments with this problem.

In canvassing this very important and much mooted subject, I think it is not necessary to try to prove that our only cause of winter loss, worthy of mention, is bee diarrhœa, for I think that all have so conceded.

The first question before us then, is what is the cause of bee diarrhœa? This disease seems to be of the intestines, caused by a too long retention of fecal accumulations. Certain it is that these accumulations could not take place unless the substance forming them was contained in the food of the bees, because chemical analysis shows the matter to be such as could come from no other source.

The next question to be solved, is whether the great variation in different colonies, regarding these accumulations, is due to difference in food or different surroundings.

The preponderance of evidence greatly favors the difference-in-food theory. Hundreds of bee-keepers have had colonies sick and dying, close beside others in perfect health, after they had fixed the conditions of temperature, humidity and ventilation, the same with all.

This gave rise to the opinion that the cause of the malady was due to "fall honey;" "boneset honey;" "sour honey;" "honey dew," etc., etc. Chemical analysis, however, proved that the fecal matter consisted mainly or entirely of pollen and water. Experience also showed that the virulence of the disease was in proportion to the predominance of pollen grains, contained in the fecal mass. These and other observations gave rise to what is known as

THE POLLEN THEORY;

a theory which is credited to the author, and has been much discussed throughout our periodicals devoted to bee-culture. I, too, had ample evidence that the cause of the disease was contained in the food, and began to ponder on the subject.

I called to mind the fact that honey was a highly oxygenized food; that pollen was as highly nitrogenized; that these two greatly varying substances, so radical in their elementary principles, were the only food for our bees, and how well the one fitted their confined state, while the other equally served their demands while growing or repairing the waste of tissue caused by exertion. I also remembered how utterly unfit was either, to serve the purpose of the other. I then grasped the idea that possibly the consumption of nitrogen in confinement, was the cause of all the trouble, and that this element was taken when the bees consumed honey (by way of its floating pollen), or in much greater proportion when they consumed bee-bread. I put this forth as a theory only, hoping that a discussion upon it would lead many others into the investigation. As time passed, and opportunity offered a partial test, more and more plausible this hypothesis appeared. Last winter gave us a chance for better testing this, as well as other theories, and I offer you the following from my experience, as bearing upon the subject.

In the autumn of 1884, I placed bees in two cellars; one containing 40, and the other 91 colonies. The old cellar containing the 40 colonies, was at all times very dry, while the new one containing the 91, was very damp. Both cellars were allowed to become quite too cold, to test the endurance of bees with sugar syrup; the temperature in the old cellar was down as low as 10 and 15 degrees above zero, in the new, damp cellar, as low as 25 degrees. The old cellar contained bees with sugar syrup only, and of its 40 colonies, all but five died, with no symptoms of diarrhœa in any hive. The new, damp cellar, containing the 91 colonies, had 73 colonies without pollen őr honey—sugar syrup only—10 colonies with little pollen, and stores of part honey and part sugar syrup, and 8 colonies having all natural stores. This cellar was so damp that mold collected on the alighting-boards and between the combs, on the under side of the covers, etc. About one-third of the colonies had upward ventilation by way of nails pushed under the board covers; the other two-thirds had no upward ventilation whatever. In numerous hives, water could be seen running out on the alighting-board. If the covers of those hives which were tight down, were lifted and turned up edgewise, water would run from them. In spring, the health of the 91 colonies stood thus: Of the 8 on natural stores, 6 died with diarrhœa, and the other 2 came out in good condition. All were treated alike with no upward ventilation. Of the 10 with little bee-bread and mixed stores, 8 lived, while 2 died. Of the remaining 73, with nothing in the combs but pure sugar syrup, not one showed any signs of diarrhœa, whatever.

I will now state how matters stood with the out-door colonies of this same home apiary. I had 49 colonies, each on 6 American frames with combs, in tenement hives, that in summer contain 19 combs, all resting horizontally. On either side of the 6 combs and bees, was a 2-inch chaff, cloth-sided division-cushion; over all, in the upper story, was a large chaff cushion, about 6 inches thick. These hives were painted white, and rested high, so that they were above the most of the snow. Twenty-five of them contained no honey, and only a cell of pollen here and there, and were well supplied with sugar syrup; 24 contained a little honey and bee-bread, and all the rest of the food was sugar syrup. I had no idea of losing any of these colonies, but in this I was in error, for every one died. Among the 25 there was scarcely a sign of disease; the combs were clean and nice. Among the other 24, there was occasional symptoms of diarrhœa, here and there, but nothing to amount to anything. I have had colonies show many times more symptoms of disease and survive, and come up strong for the June honey harvest. None of these colonies died of diarrhœa. Of what did they die? Cold, too long continued; and those in the old, cold cellar did the same. But how in a cellar? Cold is a giant in a cellar. Why? Because it continues; there is no ray of sunlight, no immediate raising of temperature, or chance for the bees to change position. What degree can bees stand? That depends upon the duration. Here is the important point that too many of us have overlooked. Forty degrees below, can be endured for a short time, but 10 to 15 degrees above, will kill bees if continued, diarrhœa or no diarrhœa.

It is the temperature within the hive, that effects the bees, and it requires time for the temperature without to effect the temperature within.

In this same yard stood 17 colonies lower down and packed warmer than the 49 just referred to, all being on full natural stores of honey and pollen, and in the regular 8-frame Langstroth hives. All but two, died. All of them had diarrhœa badly. Not until we could remove bee-diarrhœa, could we get a clear view of any other causes which might result in the death of our bees.

Just to the left stood 73 colonies packed like the above 17; these had little pollen in their combs, and stores of a mixture of sugar and honey, just the same as the 10 referred to in the new, damp cellar. They, like the 17, were low down, and were pretty well covered with snow during the severe weather. Of these 73 colonies, about one-half survived.

Of my out-apiary of 208 colonies, all packed, and all on natural stores, nearly all died.

But let us go farther. Not satisfied with this, I began sending specimens of excreta to Prof. Cook. The first specimen was excreta from a radical case of diarrhœa, with bees all dead, one among the eight which died in the new cellar. I also enclosed some pollen from the comb contained in the frame from whose top-bar I took the excreta. The Professor answered as follows: "I have subjected the pollen to a very careful examination with a one-sixth objective. I find several kinds of pollen grains, two of which are by far the most common. One is oval, rather pointed, with a longitudinal slit and numerous projections; the other is globular and thickly set with projections much like those in the other. I then studied the excreta, and had some one else made the change, I should have stoutly maintained that the objects were the same that I had just studied. The kinds of pollen were exactly the same in style and markings. The pollen you sent had been liberally appropriated by the bees whose excreta you sent."

I will here state that no attempt at breeding had been made by this colony. I will quote from another letter from Prof. Cook: "I went to a neighbor's bees, all of which are dead, and I took three with long, black, turgid bodies and dissected out their alimentary canal as before. The stomach and intestines were fairly bursting with repletion; slight pressure sent the black, odorous excreta flying. This was almost one exclusive mass of pollen-grains held in a watery mixture."

Before further considering the pollen theory, let us discuss other conditions which are supposed to bear directly upon the problem.

VENTILATION.

Notwithstanding much stress has been placed upon "pure air" for bees, I have long thought that success in wintering, rested almost entirely outside of ventilation. I have seen so many colonies come from most illy ventilated repositories, in splendid condition, and had so many reports of like nature from reliable sources, that I am forced to regard that question of minor importance.

Last winter I received a letter from Mr. Boomhower, of New York—a bee-keeper who winters his bees with greatest success—from which I quote the following:

"All ventilators to bee-cellars are a damage and amount to nothing. This has been proven to me over and over again."

In response to a question bearing directly on this subject, Prof. Cook sends me the following:

"Bees certainly use air all winter; if wintering well, very little will do—perhaps simply what is in the hive—but unless they are kept very quiet, they would need more."

In my opinion, this quietude is dependent upon temperature and food. In our Mich. State Bulletin, No. 8. the Professor, among other wise and useful instructions, presents to bee-keepers the following:

"Ventilation has also been much discussed, and various theories have been offered. Yet the physiologist, and especially the physio-entomologist, will not be easily persuaded that insects whose functional activity is so slight that a minimum of food supplies their wants, stand in need of much air. One year at the College I sealed a large colony of bees with ice frozen solid at the entrance of the hive, and yet the colony wintered exceptionally well. This colony remained for more than three months entombed in a snow bank. As the hive was glued or propolized at the top, we can see that the ventilation was slight indeed. Thus physiology and experience both show that under the best conditions, little heed need be given to ventilation. While bees do not hibernate in the sense of becoming totally inactive, yet they may and should have their vital activity kept at the minimum, else they will need air and quite ample ventilation. As we have already seen, cold or heat—that is a temperature much below or above 45 degrees F.—arouses bees, excites nutrition, and of course would necessitate more food and oxygen, and so more ventilation. Unless we can keep the bees then, in just the condition to enforce quiet, we must arrange for ample ventilation.

It goes without saying, that the temperature inside a hive, in which bees are wintering, must generally be warmer than that outside the same. The fact that bees do not hibernate, establishes this truth. The thermometer confirms it. We know that moisture is sure to collect on a cool surface; but water dripping upon bees cannot be healthful. The disturbance and the wetting would both be injurious. To winter bees then with the best success needs a covering that is not a good conductor of heat. Experiments on quite an extended scale have shown me that this is not all theory.

We see then that the requisites to success in wintering bees are: enough good food, uniform temperature without the hives at about 45 degrees F., slight ventilation. and a cover to the hive which is a non-conductor of heat."

Mr. W. H. Shirley, of Millgrove, Mich., relates an instance of his observation, where a farmer neighbor determined to smother some colonies of bees to get rid of them and to get their honey. With moist blue clay he hermetically sealed the hives. and left them for 48 hours, when he concluded the bees must be dead; but when the hives were opened, to his surprise and chagrin, they were not only alive, but showed no signs of any ill effects, whatever. This was early in the month of September.

I might occupy pages with just such instances, going to show that bees, when in a state of quietude, or repose, use almost no air at all.

I present these extreme views regarding ventilation, because I think they are correct, and that future experience will so prove them; but if your experience teaches you that I am mistaken, follow it, and go no farther with mine, than merely to experiment.

MOISTURE.

My last winter's report, above presented, again strikingly illustrates the fact that humidity is not harmful to bees, as many suppose. In all my varied experience and observation, I have been unable to discover any ill effects from dampness, of itself. From Prof. Cook's Bulletin, already referred to, I quote the following:

"It would seem that a damp atmosphere, which, as we all know, is favorable to the growth and development of fungi, and inimical to health in higher animals, would be harmful to bees. It has been found, however, that in many cases, even during the terribly disastrous winters like the past one, bees have wintered remarkably well in very damp cellars. Thus while we may presume that a very damp atmosphere is not the best, yet we may safely assert, other things being all favorable, that it of itself will not carry the seeds of mortality with it."

CONFINEMENT.

At one time a few bee-keepers were inclined to look upon confinement as the prime cause of bee diarrhœa. We have ample evidence that such cannot be true. While it is a fact that frequent flights afford opportunity for our bees to discharge any intestinal accumulations that may have taken place, yet it is a demonstrated fact that confinement need not necessarily result in an accumulation of feces. I believe it is possible to keep bees confined for one year or more, and keep them in perfect health. While in the quiescent state, time has little tendency to exhaust their vitality. Practically, the age of a bee depends upon the amount of exertion it has undergone. I have no doubt but that I could have safely kept the 73 colonies, before referred to, in the cellar, two, three, or more months longer.

In an article by Mr. Hilas D. Davis, entitled "The Wintering Problem Solved," published on page 234 of the American Bee Journal for 1885, we find the following paragraph:

"On Nov. 15, 1882, I put into the cellar a number of colonies of bees, in old hives with movable frames, which were fed on sugar syrup. By some mistake one colony was left in the cellar until June 29, 1883, when I was informed that there were bees in the cellar; and upon examination I was astonished to find the colony in a perfectly healthy condition, lively, and no traces of diarrhœa, which was remarkable, as the colony, which was a small one, had been confined about 224 days, and was removed from the cellar when my other bees were nearly done swarming. It was amusing to see what a grand flight they had after their long winter's repose."

Some of our bee-keepers believe that if our colonies do not breed late in autumn, but go into winter quarters with older bees, their chances to winter well are thereby lessened; that they are thus more liable to "Spring Dwindle." Such has not been my experience. Older bees seem more inclined to seek the desired state of repose. Mr. A. E. Manum, of Bristol, Vermont, who keeps nearly 1,000 colonies, and is very successful in wintering, writes me that he prefers to have no bees hatched later than September.

Bees do not grow old with time, but from exertion. Colonies that have not bred late have not exerted themselves like those that have. The rearing of young bees is always at the expense of the vitality of the older ones. In the quiescent state scarcely any of their vitality is lost. No matter if the youngest bee in the hive was hatched September 1st, because none were hatched later, she has preserved her vitality, hence her age, and if she passes the winter in quiescence, she will last until her hive is populous. Bees preserve their vitality (age) wonderfully during autumn, when conditions are such as to discourage breeding. The converse of this proposition is equally true.

HIBERNATION.

Do bees hibernate? My esteemed friend, Rev. W. F. Clarke, of Guelph, Ontario, who has long been interested in apiculture, and once owned and edited the American Bee Journal, surprised our fraternity by presenting in his ever clear and forcible style, what is known as "The Hibernation Theory."

We at first understood him to believe that our honey bees might, and did, when wintering successfully, enter that dormant state in which we find wasps and some other insects, and of course a lively controversy arose. By consulting "Chambers" regarding the true definition of the word, we find that the state of repose which our honey bees enter, closely borders upon hibernation. Had we so understood the meaning of the term, there would have been little to discuss, as we have for years been familiar with that quiescent state which bees assume when wintering successfully.

We do not, however, consider this quiescent, or semi-hibernating state, a cause, but an effect of successful wintering and its conditions. That bees can pass the winter in confinement, and in a state of activity, and build up to good colonies by the following summer, I have had positive proof; but such conditions do not denote perfect wintering, in my experience.

Whatever induces quiesence, also causes successful wintering, for bees in a diseased and distressed condition, will not remain quiet.

If you step out into our apiary at the approach of freezing weather and lift the cover from a hive, you will notice that the bees are snugly clustered, lying perfectly motionless. As you raise the cover, they respond by raising their abdomens and wings, but at once recline to their normal position, and should you immediately replace the cover, excluding the light and cooler air, this quiescence will continue. It is a condition induced by a certain temperature, and when that temperature changes, going either higher or lower, to a sufficient degree, just as soon as its influence is felt by the bees, they arouse to activity. If the change is to a sufficiently higher degree, they at once propose to go out, look around, and see if any useful employment can be found. If, on the other hand, the temperature falls below a certain point, the bees becoming uncomfortably cool, at once arouse and begin raising the temperature by exercising. This exertion calls for larger quantities of food, and if their food is not free from improper substances, such excessive consumption will soon overload the intestines with fecal matter, resulting in bee diarrhœa.

While it is evident that cold plays a very important part in causing this disease, yet we know there is still another cause, because we have many times witnessed perfect health in one colony, and disease in another, though sitting side by side in the same kind of hives, with like preparations and in the same repository. Where can the difference be, except in the food?

As already stated, I am quite positive that there is where it is to be found, and I believe that the difference in food, regarding its wintering qualities, depends upon the amount of nitrogen it contains. I believe that some kinds of honey, in certain seasons, contain much more nitrogen (in the form of floating pollen) than others, or the same in other seasons; and I believe this accounts, in part, for the different results we obtain when all conditions are apparently equal. It also accounts for the fact that pure cane sugar syrup (which contains no nitrogen and more oxygen than honey) has proven the best of all winter food for bees. But this is not all.

I am quite confident that when bees are exercising during their summer work, or in winter, to keep up temperature, such exercise calls for nitrogenous food, and they instinctively consume it, if within reach. By careful examination I have found that in cases where I fed sugar syrup in dry, clean combs, and left these colonies exposed to severe cold, that in every case where there was just a cell of bee-bread here and there, which was overlooked or trusted with the bees, they have emptied every one within their reach.

Bee-bread is replete with nitrogen, the tissue-making food; is mainly of pollen, and diarrhœtic excreta is composed of the same. Whether this pollen theory be correct or not, my experience bears much testimony in its favor, and I know of no other theory fully accounting for our winter losses, or I might say, bee diarrhœa, which will cover all the facts, as they have been presented to me. Certain it is that it is correct, or else the whole problem rests alone upon temperature, and in either case the directions given for always wintering safely, will insure that result.

But are all of those conditions necessary? I think not. I believe that in most seasons our bees gather honey sufficiently clear to winter upon it successfully, especially if the temperature is kept at that point which necessitates only a minimum consumption of it. I also believe that bees will not consume bee-bread during confinement, if the temperature is kept at a point that necessitates no activity on their part.

In this connection, Prof. Cook writes as follows, in the bulletin before referred to:

"If the cellar become too cold or too hot, in either case the bees become disturbed, and then I feel certain after many experiments that the bees are safer with no pollen."

They must have bee-bread to form into chime, if they rear young, whether in confinement or otherwise, but this kind of bee-bread consumption does not result in fecal accumulations. I will again quote from Prof. Cook. He says:

"The fecal mass is mostly in the intestines; sometimes it is so abundant as also to crowd the true stomach. It is not likely that the alimentary canal back of the honey stomach, and true stomach, are ever used to form the larval food; I think not, back of the sucking or honey stomach. If the pollen is used up for larval bee-food, it could not appear in the feces."

This accords with the facts connected with our experience. There are a few of our bee-keepers, some of whom are careful observers, who believe in what is known as

THE DRY-FECES THEORY,

which contemplates that bees, in healthy condition, with temperature, humidity and ventilation, all favorable, from time to time as necessity requires, discharge fecal accumulations in a dry state, and that pollen is a normal, wholesome food for bees during confinement, and is not within itself, a cause of bee diarrhœa, even when so consumed, because these frequent dry discharges prevent any excessive accumulations. Prof. Cook thinks—and my observations accord with his opinions—that bees never normally void in their hives feces that is either wet or dry. He says, that although he has made repeated examinations, he could never find dry feces in a bee.

On several occasions I have seen bees voiding (always outside of their hives) feces that was solid enough to remain in a round and elongated form, until it would dry in the sun; but these bees were always more or less diseased, though not always irrecoverably so. The colonies that I told you had nothing but pure syrup, although exposed to such a low temperature came out in spring, after a confinement of 151 days, in perfect health. Their bodies were apparently no larger than when placed in the cellar the previous autumn; on their first flight they contained nothing to void. Not a speck of anything could be found on the white hives. By carefully observing them in range with the sunlight, nothing, not even water, could be seen passing from them. As further evidence that physical exertion causes bees to consume pollen, and that pollen is what forms fecal accumulations, I will call attention to the fact that during the working season, when in harmony with this theory, bees are daily consuming larger quantities of it, if we confine them for only a short time, abdominal distention with fecal matter, always ensues.

We have now set forth many of our reasons for believing in the pollen theory, at the same time endeavoring to make it clear to the reader that whether or not we are correct regarding that belief, either in detail or the general principles of the theory, we still as firmly believe that we can winter any normal colony of bees, with as great certainty, as our horse or cow; for if that theory proves erroneous, then as already stated, I believe the problem hinges entirely upon temperature.

I will now endeavor to outline our chosen methods of complying with the laws governing success, as we believe in them and have so set forth in the foregoing. Out-door wintering can certainly boast of but two advantages; first, that it may, in favorable seasons in this latitude, allow the bees frequent flights, and second, that it saves the labor of carrying the colonies in and out of repositories. I think that I have shown that after we have secured the conditions of safe wintering, safe in all winters, no winter flights are needed, and could only effect injury to the bees, by exhausting just so much more of their vitality.

Again, if our colonies are to be left on their summer stands, we must go far south of here, before it is safe to so leave them, without extra protection, and this necessitates far more labor than that of carrying them in and out of the cellar. It is urged that a cellar or above-ground repository, costs more than packing boxes, for outside protection. This is more than offset by the value of the room for other uses in summer. Such room is just what we need. It is also argued that outside packing is very useful during spring, after all bees are on their summer stands; that it serves to prevent

"SPRING-DWINDLING."

I am confident that such dwindling is always a result of imperfect wintering, for I have never seen or heard of a case, when the bees had passed the period of confinement, in a healthy condition. I believe that bees that spring dwindle, had the diarrhœa, though in many cases the fecal accumulations were not great enough to cause evacuations in or about the hive; the same taking place away in the air.

The intestines are diseased, however, thus lessening the vitality of the bees to such an extent that they cannot survive long enough to duplicate their numbers with young bees, unless the weather is most favorable. In this locality, all healthy colonies, will, after being placed upon their summer stands, not only protect the brood they may have when set out, but also take care of all that develops from day to day, as fast as we care to have breeding progress.

(With wholesome food, and proper temperature, it is neither necessary nor advisable to remove our colonies from their repositories, where in the quiescent state they rest unconscious of the swift winged flight of time, till the struggles of winter giving place to spring, are past and flowers in bloom, affording fresh pollen and perhaps nectar, for the workers.)

If we lived in a locality where this was not the case, we should in spring, pack the top of our New Hive (the bottom of which is protected by the bottom-stand), and as it is so very shallow it would be nearly all protected. We would simply remove the cover, put on the honey board, spread a paper over this, place an empty case on top of all, fill it with saw-dust, replace the cover and the work is done. Paper and saw-dust are all the extras needed.

The evenness and height of temperature upon which that vitality-saving, quiet condition depends. cannot be maintained out-doors. I never saw a colony of bees that had wintered perfectly out-of-doors. I have wintered 500 colonies out, and saved nearly all and all came up in good condition for the honey harvest. This is not perfection however, but may be some ways from it, and toward diarrhœa and death.

(When a colony enters the quiescent state at the approach of cold weather and remains in that condition without interruption till the flowers bloom again, consuming a minimum of food, presenting abdomens no larger than when confinement began, discharging no feces on first flight, then they have wintered perfectly; but this cannot be accomplished out-doors, nor anywhere, unless the food is perfect; in my opinion, free from nitrogen—pollen.)

(My numerous experiments in out-door wintering, have led me to prefer a plan that may properly be called a combination of the clamp and packing systems.

We place our hives in a row about four inches apart, all fronting south. eight of them constituting a clamp. The front ends are about four inches from the ground, the back ends about seven inches, all on the same level. Out of some old refuse lumber, we rip some pieces two feet long and four inches wide; point these pieces at one end and drive them into the ground between the hives at their fronts, nearly on a level with the tops of the hives; get a board 18 inches wide and 12 feet long; place it on the hive edgewise, its lower edge resting just back of the stakes; select another board the same length, and 24 inches wide, placing it edgewise upon the ground six inches back of the back ends of the hives. You can now take shade-boards, or other short pieces, and nail across the ends of these boards from their top to bottom edges, when you will have your eight hives so surrounded with walls that you can pack dry sawdust, chaff, forest leaves or other suitable·non-conducting material about eight or ten inches thick at the outside of the outside hives, six inches thick behind, and five to ten inches thick over their tops. Now we lay two tiers of shade-boards, breaking joints with each other, on the top for a roof, and as the front is several inches higher than the back, the backward pitch will carry off the water. We also wedge the packing between the hives, and the stakes at their front ends hold it from running out in front. These boards may be whole, or narrow ones cleated together. As we use shade-boards for ends and roof, these flat boards are our only additional fixtures.

The tops can be packed as we prefer; either above the board covers, as glued fast by the bees, or upon the absorbant plan with covers removed and clothes laid over in their place. Now your eight hives are well packed except their fronts, which we protect as follows: We take shade boards, or we may take one continuous board, twelve feet long, and fifteen or eighteen inches wide, and lean it up against the hives and over their entrances at an angle of about forty-five degrees. This leaves a triangular opening all along in front of their entrances, which we stop up at each end with hay or straw. We now pile hay or straw all over this leaning front board and well out at the ends, reaching up as high as the top of the clamp, and about two feet out in front of the leaning board. As soon as it snows, and covers up the hay or straw, the fronts of your hives are also well protected.

But this is not all; the air furnished the hives must come in slowly, becoming more or less tempered by the earth and warmth of the clamp. Much as with cellar wintering, the air which enters the entrances of the hives, is also protected. It matters not how deep may be the snow, nor how much covered with ice, the ventilation is always ample. In locations where but little snow may be expected, I would advise making up the deficiency with greater quantities of the hay or straw.

These clamps should be formed some little time before the bees cease flying. We bring our colonies together in autumn, again spreading them apart in spring, causing them always to mark their new location by the precautions given on page 29. The front boards and hay should not be adjusted until you do not care to have your bees fly any longer. If, during the winter, favorable weather occurs, and you wish your bees to fly, pull forward your hay and front board, when the sun will immediately warm up the front ends of your hives and entrances, the front board and hay serving as an alighting place for bees that may drop down. This is our favorite out-door method of protection; still I prefer in-door wintering, and a cellar to all other repositories.

The question now arises, how shall we arrange our hives in the cellar? This problem is one that I am arranging to experiment with during the coming winter. I think it matters but little. Certain it is, that an even temperature within our hives, is preferable. The more non-conducting are they and their arrangement, the better they are for the maintainance of that even temperature. Also for a higher degree; consequently, I favor leaving the covers tight upon the hives, as sealed by the bees, pitching them forward, and leaving the entrance wide open. For our New Hives we have constructed a two inch rim, that we place under each one, thus supplying that space between the bottoms of the frames and bottom-board. Of what value this may prove, only experience can decide. It is not a new device, and while many speak in its favor, none object to it. It certainly will not produce nor prevent bee diarrhœa, but yet may be worthy of our adoption with this style of hive.

I shall pile my hives in tiers, one upon another (the strongest colonies at the bottom), as high as I can reach, placing the first tier upon the bottom of the cellar, and expect as perfect success with one tier as another, for such was my last winter's experience. We have before spoken of Repository Ventilation, and Moisture. For our coming winter's experiments our colonies will contain stores of all kinds of honey, and of pure cane sugar syrup. We feed the syrup from the large feeder described on pages 56 and 66. We prepare it as follows:

Into a boiling-pan put three pounds of water, heating it until it boils, and with a wooden paddle stir this boiling water as you sift into it ten pounds of granulated sugar. When it is all dissolved, and the syrup is boiling, pour in one-half tea-cupful of water, in which has previously been dissolved a level tea-spoonful of tartaric acid. Stir it a moment longer, and then remove it from the fire. The amount of water, acid and sugar mentioned in the above way of preparing the syrup, is given merely as a proportion. I boil half a barrel of sugar at one time, on a common cook-stove, in a flat copper boiler made for the purpose, and which covers the entire top of the stove. Feed the syrup while warm (not hot). if convenient.

It will not crystallize if the acid is used in the proportion mentioned, is of full strength, and the syrup boiled as directed. It is at once, when cool, of the consistency of well-ripened honey, and as the bees receive, store and seal it readily, I know of no reason why it is best to feed it thinner, and depend upon them to evaporate out a portion of the water. \

The best time to feed the syrup is at once—as soon as you are satisfied that all gathering of natural stores is past.

In the chapters on "Hives" we described our method of management, that brought our colonies out at the close of honey-gathering in a condition to feed, without first having to extract honey from their combs. In this chapter I have also mentioned exchanging empty combs for their full ones, and feeding syrup into them, in cases where the contraction system was not practiced.

I do not like this plan nearly as well as the summer method of keeping natural stores out of the brood-chamber, as it increases labor and exposure to robbers. It also frequently necessitates feeding too late in the season.

I think that when for any reason the bee-keeper desires to winter his bees upon natural stores, the method of selecting such stores, as given in the chapter on the New Hive, is a very good one to practice.

Some twelve years ago we used bows over the frames, to admit of winter passage-ways for the bees, but were never positive that they were of any value. Neither am I sure that absorbants over our bees in winter are advantageous. Drs. Southard & Ranney of Kalamazoo, Mich., who are very successful in out-door wintering, practice packing chaff over their board covers glued tightly by the bees. They also give very little lower ventilation. During the past severe winter of 1884–5, they carried their large apiary through with almost no loss.

All of our colonies in the New Hives are now in our bee-cellar, each in one case. About one-half of the hives have the narrow rims under them, and one-half are without them. All are wintering perfectly. It is a pleasure to carry these light, fixed-frame hives into the cellar.

This chapter, like the book in general, is written from the standpoint of my own latitude and experience, and while I disclaim a perfect understanding of the problem, I do believe we have practically mastered it.

CHAPTER XXVI.

Adopting Apiculture.

When one has decided to adopt bee-keeping as a business, the question may then well be asked, "how shall I commence?" I will give you my opinions regarding the subject—opinions based on experience.

In these remarks I shall suppose that the sole purpose of adopting our pursuit, is that of making money at a reasonably agreeable calling. For all other classes I have nothing to say. But now let me consider the best way to get properly started in the business. With this, like all other pursuits, the very first acquisition needed is a knowledge of its laws and principles. With this knowledge you will know how to choose a good field. You will know enough to choose one that is unoccupied, and that you can likely hold sole possession of. Besides these basic principles, you will have an understanding of the detail manipulation of the apiary.

Now, in my judgment, the best way to get possession of this knowledge, which is absolutely necessary to success, is to do just as you would if you were going to practice law, ship building, rearing silk worms or speckled trout, viz: Engage yourself with some experienced and successful man of the same calling, and with him and his fixtures study the business both in theory and practice. You will get your theory from the best literature upon the subject, and social converse with your employer. This will increase your talent. You will get your practical knowledge, made up of thousands of methods, styles and movements, by working at the business and among his fixtures. That knowledge will increase your tact. Now, the reason why I suggested the successful man only, is because this tact is usually found in company with success—in fact it is a parent of success, and is to a considerable degree catching, and the ways and means adopted by the man of tact, are authors of success.

During this apprenticeship you must mingle your thought with your labor in a proper degree, for in this business you are as much a student as an apprentice. After you have spent one or two seasons (according to your aptitude) in this way, you are competent to start in the business, with a capital that will support you and yours, and command your best mental and physical efforts, for most of the year. If you have not the capital, you are fitted to command wages in advance of the common laborer, and if acquaintance has inspired your employer with full faith in your integrity, you can likely get all the capital you need, to accompany your strength and skill. Many offer bees for sale, but I want to tell you that if I could get competent, honest men to work for me, at wages hinted at above, or work an apiary on shares, I could make more by not selling a bee, but placing my surplus stocks in another unoccupied field, with this employe to handle them.

I give it as my solemn conviction, that no man should ever attempt this business that has failed in all others in which he has been engaged. That bees do not "work for nothing and board themselves;" that "small children" and "invalids" are not eminently adapted to honey production. Experience has taught me that if there is any business in this world that demands industry, skill and tact, to insure success, it is this of ours. By attending conventions, visiting bee-keepers, and entertaining many who visit me, I have learned that successful apiarists, as a class, are more than ordinarily wide awake and intelligent.

The beginner almost invariably wants to know how many pounds of surplus honey he may expect from a hive, in a good season. Why don't he ask how many pounds in a bad one? Really, why don't he say how much is honey worth on the markets of the world? Is it likely to hold up to that figure? How much do you think it costs to produce honey per ton? Do you know of any good, unoccupied fields? About how many pounds of surplus do you think such a field would yield annually, on an average? What would be the best number of colonies to keep to secure it? and a whole lot of such questions as these.

Now, honor bright, would not these questions be more likely to be correctly answered by some experienced producer than any one else? If I should hear a young man asking questions like these, I would feel sure that he had served at least a year with some experienced apiarist, and not in vain, either.

I believe that no business is less adapted to becoming a side issue or adjunct to some other, than this of ours. On the other hand, I think it will become a specialty with the successful ones, and these men will be men of energy, intelligence and tact.

The days of dabbling along with two or four colonies; picking up bee wisdom; throwing away one and making another style of hive every year, are nearly over.

Seventeen years ago I began bee-keeping in this way. The production of honey has increased many fold since that time, and the profits of the same have greatly decreased. Had they been no greater then than now, I think my attempts at apiculture would have proven a failure. I am positive that had I then apprenticed myself to some such successful apiarist as Adam Grimm, whom it is said cleared $10,000 in one year, from his large apiaries, I would, ere this, have no further need for bees, nor their product.

For years past our state agricultural college has had, attached to the general course, an experimental apiary, conducted by Prof. A. J. Cook, our state professor of entomology; a gentleman whom, I believe, stands at the head of his profession, and is very enthusiastic regarding this part of it—the honey bee. While this school offers a fine opportunity for certain kinds of experiments, as well as thoroughly learning the physiology and character of bees, I cannot conceive that it offers as great advantages for at once learning how to produce honey at a profit, as does the large, practical apiary. It might be well, for those who are able, to take two courses in the study of our pursuit: first, at the Agricultural College and then in the apiary; but if, for any reason, only one course can be taken, I must say that I consider the practical apiary course not only first choice, but almost a necessity. For four or five years past, Mr. D. A. Jones, of Canada, and myself, have received from many times the number of applications, a limited number of

STUDENT-APPRENTICES,

and this experience has the better qualified me to judge of its benefits. We are, however, not alone in our ideas of the immense advantages of such a course. The constant solicitations received for skillful help in the apiary, and that, too, from our most successful apiarists, argues plainly that these men are of the same opinion. Neither are these opinions confined to our own land; for I have repeatedly had applications for my students from foreign countries. Very few of these calls could be satisfactorily answered, for whatever may be the student's idea, when soliciting a situation in the apiary, he is sure to embark in the business for himself if by any possibility he can command the necessary capital.

This is not the only evidence of the favorable opinions of our most successful bee-keepers. I will quote from four of our noted producers and writers. Mr. W. Z. Hutchinson says:

"If a man wishes to engage in bee-keeping as a specialty, and make money out of it, he cannot do better than to take a season's instruction with a practical apiarist in a practical working apiary."

Dr. C. C. Miller of Illinois says that "whoever purposes to make bee-keeping a business, may save himself years of discomfiture and failure, by spending a season in the apiary, as an apprentice."

Mr. E. J. Oatman of the same state, also a large and most successful honey producer, says: "I would rather, by far, employ a man after such a season's schooling, than take him after his futile efforts of five years of independent experiment."

Rev. W. F. Clarke, before referred to, a man to whom nature and years have given a keen insight into the affairs of life, says that he "should like to have just such a chance to learn the business, and should try to get it, were he not parson, and editor as to life-work."

While I can most heartily recommend a season spent in the practical working apiary, with a successful honey producer and competent teacher, as being the best and cheapest way to become a successful apiarist, I am far from urging any person to enter our already well filled ranks.

Could I accomplish the aim of this little work, viz: lend material aid to those now in the business, both in multiplying their colonies by successfully wintering, and increasing their honey crop by way of improved implements and methods, it is my opinion that there would soon be produced all the honey that consumers will pay for at a price making its production worthy of our attention. Before concluding, I will repeat, that I am firmly convinced that only the energetic, faithful, and intelligent, will be apt to succeed as honey producers.

If you possess these qualifications and thoroughly learn the business, these important truths will be your warranty of success. You will have but a limited number of mankind as competitors, and these will be men who are not willing and do not need to devote their mental and physical energy to that which yields a precarious income.

CHAPTER XXVII.
Books and Periodicals.

As a factor in the development and progress of the world's industries, the books and periodicals devoted thereto have, in modern times played an important part. I know of no industry, however humble, that has not a special literature of its own devoted to the advancement of the financial interest of those therein engaged. In the light of the accumulated experience and practical knowledge of those engaged in any business, substantial and steady progress is made. Our own chosen pursuit is no exception to this rule, but is rather a striking confirmation of it, for the almost wonderful advance in apicultural science during the past two decades, is largely due to the interchange of thought and experiment through the medium of our bee-periodicals.

At the head of our apistical literature, both in point of age of publication and mature practical thought, stands the "American Bee-Journal," as bright and fresh and newsy as when the master hand of Samuel Wagner was at the editorial helm. In tracing the career of this Journal back to its birth in 1860, I find that it has been an earnest advocate of the right, and has ever striven for the best interest of its patrons. No childish prattle or selfish hurrah-boy enthusiasm, seeking to augment the already crowded ranks of a pursuit with a class of people whose embarkation therein meant failure and financial ruin to themselves and embarrassment to those already embarked, has marked its course. A remittance of $1.00 to Thos. G. Newman & Son, 925 West Madison St., Chicago,

Ill., will secure its weekly visits for one year, and I know of no investment in bee-literature that will pay such satisfactory dividends to the intelligent apiarist.

"Gleanings in Bee-Culture," is published semi-monthly at Medina, Ohio, by A. I. Root; price $1.00 per year. Although younger in years than the American Bee-Journal (just mentioned) Gleanings is a valuable addition to our periodicals, and well worth its subscription price.

The "Bee-Keepers' Magazine," by Aspinwall & Treadwell, 16 Thomas St., N. Y.—is a regular visitor, and I should not like to dispense with it. Monthly, at $1.00 per year.

There are several other American publications of more or less note and vitality, which do not reach me, hence I have no knowledge of their special claims to public patronage.

Just over the line, in the "Queen's Dominions," D. A. Jones, of Beeton, Ontario, has started the weekly "Canadian Bee-Journal," at $1.00 per year, which gives promise of usefulness to its readers.

BOOKS.

"The Hive and Honey Bee," by Father Langstroth, and the "Mysteries of Bee-Keeping," by Father M. Quimby, were the pioneer works, from which modern apiculture has sprung. To the labors of these two veteran apiarists, are we all indebted for the inception of scientific methods and devices, which have placed our pursuit upon a substantial, practical basis, immeasurably in advance of the empiricism of the past. No practical system had been formulated by their predecessors; definite results were unknown.

In more recent years, the accumulated results attained by the fraternity have been preserved for us in such admirable books as Prof. A. J. Cook's "Manual of the Apiary," Mr. Thos. G. Newman's "Bees and Honey," King's "Bee-Keeper's Text Book," Mr. A. I. Root's "A, B, C, of Bee-Culture," Mr. L. C Root's "Quimby's New Bee-Keeping," Chas. Dadant's little pamphlet upon "Extracted Honey," Mr. Henry Alley's "Handy Book," particularly devoted to queen rearing, etc.

Odds and Ends.

[Under this head, I have grouped a few facts, either not mentioned elsewhere in these pages, or which seem to be deserving of the emphasis of repetition.]

It hath been said by him of olden time, "keep your stocks strong;" but I say unto you, "don't let your colonies remain queenless."

A friend asks me: "Have you ever mixed bees from different queens, with a view of increasing their vigor and energy as honey gatherers? If not, try exchanging frames of hatching brood, and note the result."

There is a vast difference in the quality of the tinned wire, used in wiring foundation in brood frames; that which is soft and pliable being much better than the hard, brittle "variety."

Have you ever, in your visions of the "sweet bye and bye," caught glimpses of that elysian "field" where the industrious gatherer of propolis shall find his "occupation gone," and the "wicked (bee) cease from troubling?" If so, just lubricate all hive bearings with tallow, rubbing it well into the wood, and enjoy the luxury of removing covers. supers, honey cases, etc., in the "twinkling of an eye," without a snap, jar or bee-protest.

It is good policy to keep hives well painted. The mineral paints, with the addition of a little white lead, make the cheapest and most durable coating for hives, of which we have any knowledge.

The term, "bee-space," does not only denote a space that will admit of the passage of a bee, but it refers to that space in which bees are least inclined to build brace-combs or place propolis, or bee-glue; which is a scant ⅜ of an inch.

The wire embedder, illustrated on page 63, is the invention of C. M. Ruland, Rockton, Ill.

The business of honey producing has never received the respect that it merits, neither from our government nor many of her individual members. While we are glad to be able to say that we are each year receiving more and more of the respect and attention we have long deserved; still we are at all times liable to unjust encroachments upon our industry; because, until quite recently, bee-keeping has not been a business of any importance. To protect ourselves against these unjust legal attacks, we have formed a Bee-Keepers' Union which, it seems to me, all friends of the pursuit should join. For particulars, address Thos. G. Newman, Manager, 925, W. Madison St., Chicago.

———

If judgment be used in selecting material and manufacturing hives, very excellent ones can be made out of second or third class lumber. It is not wise, and I believe not common, to use first class boards in the manufacture of first class hives. The same is true regarding the workmanship; while it should be good, all pieces being smooth and accurately cut, it is bad economy to spend the time required to smooth and polish a hive until it resembles cabinet work.

———

I wish to impress the reader's mind with the following sentiments, which I feel positive are truths:

First, beyond the matter of food, the problem of safely wintering bees rests almost wholly with temperature. Second, bees winter as safely upon shallow as upon deep combs. Third, they build combs and fill them with honey as readily and speedily in our smallest surplus receptacles, as in our largest ones.

———

I think we may correctly say that a honey field, or apiarian area, is one ordinarily nearly circular, having a diameter of nearly six miles; the apiary located at its center. I think we may call an area occupied when it contains a bee-keeper who keeps, or intends to keep within it, one-hundred or more colonies. I feel that I cannot too strongly urge you not to attempt bee-keeping within an already occupied area.

GENERAL INDEX.

PAGE

Apiculture, little connection
with farming.... 9
better for blacksmith...... 9
adopting................... 118
how to adopt........118, 119, 120
who should adopt.......119, 120
American Bee-Journal........13, 16
price reduced.............. 122
Alley, Henry................... 23
After swarms, prevention of..23, 24
Acid in winter stores........... 35
to prevent crystalization.... 36
Artificial pasturage........... 43
when it pays............... 42
what plants pay best.......43, 44
Adulteration
different opinions on........ 46
Adulterate, bee keepers do not.. 46
it does not pay to.......... 46
Apiarian supply-trade......... 49
what stimulated the.......50, 51
requires tact, energy and perseverance to be successful
lu.................... 50
Apiarian implements.......... 52
who should make.......... 49
who should buy........... 49
illy constructed........... 49
by freight.................51, 52
by express.................51. 52
Apiarian supplies
how to order..............50, 51
A B C of Bee Culture.... ......*.. 122
Aspinwall and Treadwell....... 122
Bee-keeping, as a business....... 7
can be made a success....... 7
in a small way............. 8
as a specialty.............. 8
as related to mechanics..... 8
for women................. 10
Bees, age of worker.......... 12
varieties of.............12, 13, 14
crossing the races.........14, 15
value of.................. 16
on shares.................16, 17
subduing................. 17
careless handling of........ 18
scared by smoke.......... 18
size of...................22, 23
how to make them mark new
locations................. 29
Bee enemies................... 38
diseases.................... 38
paralysis.................. 38
moths....................38, 40
smoker.................... 52

smoker, fuel for........53, 57, 58
best size of................ 53
Bingham's the best.......... 53
cut of..................... 57
veil (see protectors)
tent...................... 55
conveniences of........... 56
size and construction of..... 56
objections to.............. 56
Bee-space, its great value......78, 79
what is it?................. 123
Father Langstroth's inven-
tion....................78, 79
Bee-diarrhœa...............107, 108
Bee-keeper's Magazine......... 122
"Bees and Honey"............ 122
"Bee keeper's Text Book".... 122
Bees mixed from various hives.. 123
Books and periodicals.......... 121
Boomhower, Mr............... 109
Bingham T. F..............52, 81
Birds as enemies............. 38
Breeding, how stimulated....... 35
Capping combs................ 14
Cyprian bees.............12, 13, 15
Carniolan bees...........12, 13, 15
Cook, Prof. A. J., 4, 109, 110, 113, 120
122
Crates (see shipping crates)....49, 71
cut of.... 71
Comb-foundation....54, 60, 61, 62, 63
prefer Given.............. 61
great advantages of.......54, 62
weight of................. 54
how fastened....54, 61, 62, 63. 67
Contracting L. hive........82, 83, 103
advantages of.............82, 83
illustrated................. 83
dummies for.............82, 83
Colonies, strong. 123
how kept strong...........84, 85
Confinement................ 111
Clarke, Rev. W. F...........112, 120
Canadian Bee-Journal.......... 122
Division of labor.............. 8
Drone cells................. 11
Drones, time required to devel-
ope...................... 11
their use.................. 11
age of.................... 12
selection of............... 26
Dzierzon.................... 39
Dadant, Chas. & Son.........60, 102
Dadant's "Extracted Honey"... 122
Doolittle, G. M............81, 83, 84
Davis, Hilas D................ 111

Dry fœces theory...........113, 114
Extractor, honey.............7, 58
  many styles of.............. 53
  prefer upright gearing for... 59
  for the special list........... 59
  excelsior.................... 59
  for new hive............ 104
  prefer large can............. 60
  wax, cut of................. 70

False inducements............. 10
Fertile workers, when they appear......................... 33
  look like others............. 33
  how they lay in the cells.... 33
  prove a great annoyance.... 33
  how to get rid of.........33, 34
Feeding....................... 34
  to promote breeding......... 34
  for winter stores............ 34
  sugar syrup.............. 35
  honey to finish sections... 35, 36
  stimulative.................. 35
Feeders..................56, 57, 66
  old style, cut of............ 66
  new style, cut of............ 66
Foul blood.............38, 39, 40
  Dzierzon's remedy.......... 39
  fast spreading............... 40
  Italians less liable to......39, 40
  how developed.............. 40
  how cured............. .....39, 40
Fountain pump a necessity....20, 55
  Whitman's................55, 70
  for hiving swarms...... ... 55
  will last a lifetime.......... 55
  illustrated.................. 70
  perfectly made............. 70
  for washing windows..... . 71
  cleaning buggies........... 71
  for lawns and gardens 71
  for extinguishing fires...... 71

German bees.....12, 13, 14, 15, 21. 28
Given press illustrated....:...... 61
  makes best foundation....60, 61
Gleanings in Bee Culture....... 122

Honey, early price of........... 7
  raising for one's own use.... 7
  comb or extracted, which pays best..............44, 45
  as a sauce.............. 47
  in quantity...... 47
  keep local demand supplied with.................... 47
  ripe....................... 45
  extracted............ 45
  comb...........45, 48, 49
  styles of packages for.....48, 49
Honey-knife, Bingham's.. ...53, 68
  cut of.................... 68

patented.................... 68
Hive, improved Langstroth..... 77
  cut of.... 77
  bottom stand for.... 77
  honey board for............ 77
  readily movable............ 81
  small brood chamber preferable.................... 81
  contraction of (see contraction)
  our new illustrated.......... 89
  brood chamber of horizontal sections............ 89, 90
  frames for................. 90
  reversible... ....90, 99
  surplus cases for.........91, 93
  case illustrated............. 91
  honey-board 91, 93
  bottom board illustrated.... 92
  bottom stand for, illustrated 92
  size of parts.......90, 91, 92, 93
  wide frames for, cut of 93
  description of............93, 94
  surplus cases for, reversible 93
  how contracted...........94, 98
  how enlarged.............. 95
  Father Langstroth on shallow.... 95
  for winter 95, 96
  to fit former case to......... 98
  general management of..... 99
  seldom need opening....... 100
  finding green in............ 100
  clipping queen cells in...... 100
  bees easily handled in....... 101
  shade for....... 101
  for extracted honey.....102, 103
  quickly manipulated 99, 103, 105
  for extra honey flow 104
  honey extractor for.. 104
  should be made from sample only...................... 105
  must be made accurately.... 105
  patented................... 105
  tested by Hutchinson....... 106
Honey board, cuts of.......... 77
  description of............77, 78
  queen excluding............ 78
  new style illustrated........ 91
  new style reversible 91
  new style described....... . 93
  to control swarming......... 104
"Handy Book," Alley's......... 122
Hibernation................. 112
Hybrid bees.;............13, 14, 15
Hutchinson, W. Z., 24, 61, 78, 84, 99, 106, 120
Improvements. 8
Italian bees............13, 14, 15, 21
Increase 19
  artificial 20
  plan No. 1................20, 21

plan No. 2................20, 21
prevention of.............22, 23
Italianizing..............31 32
Jones, D. A.............120, 122
Lamp nursury................28, 55
keeps uniform temperature 27
large uniform queens come
from.....................27
cut of.....................69
Langstroth, Father (of modern
apiculture)............42, 122
hive and honey bee......42, 122

Mixed husbandry............. 8
Maloney, George........... 13
My friend, 4, 19, 20, 21, 25, 26, 27, 31
33, 34, 36, 37, 47, 48, 50, 51, 52
53, 54, 55, 56, 57
Mellilot clover............43, 44
Marketing in old times.......... 47
in modern.............47, 48, 49
through commission men... 48
too early................. 49
Market distant............47, 48
home...................47, 48
preparing for.............. 48
when to................... 48
Manum, A. E................ 111
Miller, C. C................ 120
"Mysteries of Bee-keeping".... 122
"Manual of the Apiary"........ 122

Natural history............. 11
Nature a blind force......... 12
faulty................... 12
Nuclei.................... 20
forming.................28, 29
Newman, Thos. G........4, 43, 122
Newman, Thos. G. & Son....59, 121

Osborn, A. W................ 13
Overstocking, but little known
about..................41, 42
statistical reports on....... 42
Opening hives unnecessarily, 99, 100
Oatman, E. J................ 120
Odds and Ends............... 123

Price of honey fluctuates....... 10
Physiology, bee.............. 11
Pleurisy, excellent honey plant, 28
43, 44
Protectors, face...........55, 69
illustrated............... 69
material for...........55, 69
convenience of..........55, 69
best color for............. 69
when to wear them........ 55
Patents are they necessary...... 73
evidence of civilization. 73
a necessity............... 74

best for all................74, 75
favored by Father Lang-
stroth.................... 75
Pollen theory.........107, 108, 109
Propolis, how avoided......... 123
Paint for hives............... 123

Queen, fertile................ 11
cages, how made........... 55
her capacity.............. 11
eggs of, when they hatch... 11
cells, position of.......... 11
at will................... 28
how fertilized............. 11
price of.................. 16
clipping wings of.......... 25
rearing,...25, 26, 27, 28, 29, 30, 31
Queen-rearing
under swarming impulse.... 27
artificial................. 26
our preferred method. 27, 28, 29
30, 31
Queens to breed from.......... 27
prolificness of...........84, 85
cost of.................84, 85
introducing virgin.......... 30
danger in introducing....... 30
introducing fertile......... 31
Quimby, M...........26, 39, 52, 122

Reversible-frames...........21, 85
cuts of...............62, 86, 87,
Reversing, advantages of........
Ruland, C. M................ 123
Root, A. I....28, 43, 54, 64, 102, 122
Removing bees............... 29
Robbing, how encouraged....36, 37
how to prevent...........36, 37
Register, honey..........54, 64, 101
illustrated................. 64
how used...............64, 65
queen 54, 55, 64
wood block preferable 55
how to record....... 55

Specialty...............8, 9
Supply and demand........... 10
Success demands, tact and in-
dustry.................... 10
Syrian bees...............12, 13
Subduing bees............... 17
Smoking bees............... 18
Smoke not harmful........... 18
Swarming................... 19
natural objectionable 19
Swarms, natural how to manage 20
prevention of.........22, 23, 24
Shipping crates, small sell best, 49
56
small, ship safer........ .49, 56
Smoker (see bee-smoker)
Sections, surplus............. 54
advantages of reversing...... 97

½ ℔.............................. 49
sizes of...................54, 63
best wood for.... ....54, 64
all dove-tail preferred....... 54
4¼x4¼ a standard......... 63
Separators...................... 54
Screen house... ....56, 65
how made and used.......56, 65
why better than tent......56, 65
prevents robbing..........56 65
Surplus case, cut of............ 77
description of.............79, 80
how tiered up......... 80
Heddon's old 96, 97
"   new............... 91
two story objectionable....96, 97
advantages of tiering 87
Shade for hives................. 101
Shirley, W. H............... 110
Spring dwindling 114
causes of................... 115
Student-apprentices............ 120

Terry, T. B.................... 8
Temperature for green rearing. 28
Transferring, old method....... 32

modern.................. 32, 33

Unoccupied fields.............. 10

Vick, James.................. 8
Varieties of bees.............. 12
Ventilation 109, 110

Wintering, the problem solved, 106
in cellar.................114. 115
out door..............115, 116. 117
feeding for....,............ 117
absorbents for.............. 118
pollen theory........107, 108. 109
experiments in, 107, 108, 109, 111
breeding.................... 109
moisture.................110, 111
ventilation 109, 110
confinement 111
old bees for................111
hibernation.............110, 112
temperature for, 106, 108, 110,
[112 to 118
Worker cells.................. 11
Wiring tool (cut)...........63, 123
Wire for frames.............63, 123

INDEX TO CHAPTERS.

           PAGE
Artificial Pasturage.... .... 43 to 44
Adulteration.. 46 to 47
Apiarian Supply Trade........................... 49 to 52
Apiarian Implements........................... 52 to 72
Adopting Apiculture ... .118 to 121
Bee-Keeping as a Business .... 7 to 10
Bees on Shares........ .... 16 to 17
Bee-Enemies.. 38 to 40
Books and Periodicals.... ....121 to 122
Comb or Extracted Honey?........................... 44 to 45
Fertile-Workers .... 33 to 34
Feeding.......................... 34 to 36
Hives .... 76 to 87
Hives, New................................ 88 to 106
Italianizing........................ 31 to 32
Increase................................ 19 to 25
Marketing............................ 47 to 49
Natural History................................ 11 to 12
Overstocking........................... 41 to 43
Patents; Are They Necessary? .... 73 to 75
Queen-Rearing... .... 25 to 31
Robbing........................... 36 to 37
Subduing Bees.......................... 17 to 19
Transferring.... .... 32 to 33
Varieties of Bees .. .. 12 to 15
Value of Bees 16
Wintering........................106 to 118

www.ingramcontent.com/pod-product-compliance
Lightning Source LLC
Chambersburg PA
CBHW030616270326
41927CB00007B/1192